NIST Special Publication 800-68
Revision 1

Guide to Securing Microsoft Windows XP Systems for IT Professionals: A NIST Security Configuration Checklist

Recommendations of the National Institute of Standards and Technology

Karen Scarfone
Murugiah Souppaya
Paul M. Johnson

COMPUTER SECURITY

Computer Security Division
Information Technology Laboratory
National Institute of Standards and Technology
Gaithersburg, MD 20899-8930

October 2008

U.S. Department of Commerce

Carlos M. Gutierrez, Secretary

National Institute of Standards and Technology

Dr. Patrick D. Gallagher, Deputy Director

Reports on Computer Systems Technology

The Information Technology Laboratory (ITL) at the National Institute of Standards and Technology (NIST) promotes the U.S. economy and public welfare by providing technical leadership for the nation's measurement and standards infrastructure. ITL develops tests, test methods, reference data, proof of concept implementations, and technical analysis to advance the development and productive use of information technology. ITL's responsibilities include the development of technical, physical, administrative, and management standards and guidelines for the cost-effective security and privacy of sensitive unclassified information in Federal computer systems. This Special Publication 800-series reports on ITL's research, guidance, and outreach efforts in computer security and its collaborative activities with industry, government, and academic organizations.

> Certain commercial entities, equipment, or materials may be identified in this document in order to describe an experimental procedure or concept adequately. Such identification is not intended to imply recommendation or endorsement by the National Institute of Standards and Technology, nor is it intended to imply that the entities, materials, or equipment are necessarily the best available for the purpose.

Acknowledgements

The authors, Karen Scarfone and Murugiah Souppaya of the National Institute of Standards and Technology (NIST) and Paul M. Johnson of Booz Allen Hamilton, wish to thank their colleagues who reviewed drafts of this document and contributed to its technical content, particularly Tim Grance and Blair Heiserman of NIST and Kurt Dillard.

Acknowledgements, Original Version

The authors, Murugiah Souppaya of the National Institute of Standards and Technology (NIST) and Karen Kent and Paul M. Johnson of Booz Allen Hamilton, wish to thank their colleagues who reviewed drafts of this document and contributed to its technical content. The authors would like to acknowledge Chris Enloe, Tim Grance, Arnold Johnson, Larry Keys, Kathy Ton-nu, and John Wack of NIST; Robert Chang, Anthony Harris, and Richard Park of Booz Allen Hamilton; and Kurt Dillard of Microsoft for their keen and insightful assistance throughout the development of the document. The authors would also like to express their thanks to the reviewers of the draft publication for their particularly valuable comments and suggestions, in particular Dean Farrington (Wells Fargo Bank), Nathan Look (Los Angeles Department of Water and Power), James McKeithen, W. Warren Pearce (Air Force Satellite Control Network), Peter Tracy (Belarc), the Department of Energy, the Internal Revenue Service, and the Social Security Administration. Additionally, the authors also thank the Department of Homeland Security (DHS), Defense Information Agency (DISA), the Center for Internet Security (CIS), the National Security Agency (NSA), the United States Air Force (USAF), Microsoft Corporation, and other individuals for their valuable contributions to the baseline security templates and continued hard work to improve security in this and other similar efforts.

The National Institute of Standards and Technology would also like to express its appreciation and thanks to the Department of Homeland Security for its sponsorship and support of NIST SP 800-68.

Trademark Information

Microsoft, Windows, Windows Vista, Windows XP, Windows 2000, Windows NT, Internet Explorer, Microsoft Office, Outlook, Outlook Express, and Microsoft Word are either registered trademarks or trademarks of Microsoft Corporation in the United States and other countries.

All other names are registered trademarks or trademarks of their respective companies.

Table of Contents

Executive Summary ES-1

1. Introduction 1-1
    1.1 Authority 1-1
    1.2 Purpose and Scope 1-1
    1.3 Audience 1-2
    1.4 Document Structure 1-2

2. Windows XP Security Guide Development 2-1
    2.1 Windows XP System Roles and Requirements 2-2
    2.2 Security Categorization of Information and Information Systems 2-3
    2.3 Baseline Security Controls and Threat Analysis Refinement 2-4
        2.3.1 Local Threats 2-5
        2.3.2 Remote Threats 2-7
    2.4 Environments and Security Controls Documentation 2-10
        2.4.1 SOHO 2-10
        2.4.2 Enterprise 2-11
        2.4.3 Specialized Security-Limited Functionality (SSLF) 2-13
        2.4.4 Legacy 2-14
        2.4.5 FDCC 2-14
        2.4.6 Security Documentation 2-14
    2.5 Implementation and Testing of Security Controls 2-15
    2.6 Monitoring and Maintenance 2-15
    2.7 Summary of Recommendations 2-16

3. Windows XP Security Components Overview 3-1
    3.1 New Features in Windows XP 3-1
        3.1.1 Networking Features 3-1
        3.1.2 Authentication and Authorization 3-2
        3.1.3 Other 3-4
    3.2 Security Features Inherited from Windows 2000 3-5
        3.2.1 Kerberos 3-5
        3.2.2 Smart Card Support 3-6
        3.2.3 Internet Connection Sharing 3-6
        3.2.4 Internet Protocol Security 3-6
        3.2.5 Encrypting File System 3-7
    3.3 Summary of Recommendations 3-7

4. Installation, Backup, and Patching 4-1
    4.1 Performing a New Installation 4-1
        4.1.1 Partitioning Advice 4-1
        4.1.2 Installation Methods 4-2
    4.2 Backing Up Systems 4-4
    4.3 Updating Existing Systems 4-5
        4.3.1 Update Notification 4-5
        4.3.2 Microsoft Update Types 4-5
        4.3.3 Automatic Updates 4-6
        4.3.4 Microsoft Update 4-7

        4.3.5   Patching in Managed Environments 4-9
   4.4   Identifying Security Issues 4-10
   4.5   Summary of Recommendations 4-11

5. Overview of the Windows XP Security Policy Configuration and Templates 5-1

   5.1   Windows XP Security Templates 5-1
   5.2   Analysis and Configuration 5-2
   5.3   Group Policy Distribution 5-3
   5.4   Administrative Templates 5-5
   5.5   Summary of Recommendations 5-6

6. NIST Windows XP Template and GPO Settings Overview 6-1

   6.1   Account Policies 6-1
   6.2   Local Policies 6-2
        6.2.1   Audit Policy 6-3
        6.2.2   User Rights Assignment 6-4
        6.2.3   Security Options 6-4
   6.3   Event Log Policies 6-5
   6.4   Restricted Groups 6-5
   6.5   System Services 6-5
   6.6   File Permissions 6-7
   6.7   Registry Permissions 6-8
   6.8   Registry Values 6-8
        6.8.1   Automatic Functions 6-8
        6.8.2   Networking 6-9
        6.8.3   Other Template Settings 6-10
        6.8.4   Settings Not In the NIST Templates 6-11
   6.9   Summary of Recommendations 6-12

7. Additional Windows XP Configuration Recommendations 7-1

   7.1   Filesystem Security 7-1
        7.1.1   NTFS 7-1
        7.1.2   Folder Options 7-2
        7.1.3   Show Hidden File Types 7-3
        7.1.4   EFS 7-4
        7.1.5   Storage Device Sanitization and Disposal 7-6
   7.2   User Accounts and Groups 7-7
        7.2.1   Built-in Accounts 7-7
        7.2.2   Built-in Groups 7-9
        7.2.3   Daily Use Accounts 7-10
        7.2.4   Local Session Protection 7-11
        7.2.5   Password Reset Disk 7-12
   7.3   Auditing 7-13
        7.3.1   Individual File Auditing 7-13
        7.3.2   Reviewing Audit Logs 7-14
        7.3.3   Time Synchronization 7-15
   7.4   Software Restriction Policy 7-15
   7.5   Securing Network Interfaces 7-17
        7.5.1   Unneeded Networking Components 7-17
        7.5.2   Use of Port 445 7-18
        7.5.3   TCP/IP Configuration 7-18

7.6	Windows Firewall	7-19
7.7	IPsec	7-21
7.8	Wi-Fi Network Configuration	7-23
7.9	Memory Files	7-24
7.10	Summary of Recommendations	7-24

8. Application Security Configuration Recommendations 8-1

8.1	Productivity Application Suites	8-1
8.2	Web Browsers	8-2
8.3	E-mail Clients	8-2
8.4	Personal Firewalls	8-3
8.5	Antivirus Software	8-3
8.6	Antispyware Software	8-4

9. Putting It All Together 9-1

List of Appendices

Appendix A— Federal Agency Security Configurations A-1

Appendix B— Windows XP Service Pack 3 Security B-1

Appendix C— Mapping Windows XP Controls to NIST SP 800-53 .... C-1

C.1	Management Controls	C-1
C.2	Operational Controls	C-2
C.3	Technical Controls	C-7

Appendix D— Commonly Used TCP/IP Ports on Windows XP Systems D-1

Appendix E— Tools E-1

Appendix F— Resources F-1

F.1	Vulnerability Databases	F-1
F.2	Mailing Lists	F-1
F.3	Print Resources	F-1
F.4	Related NIST Documents and Resources	F-2
F.5	Microsoft Web-Based Resources	F-3
	F.5.1 General Windows XP Resources	F-3
	F.5.2 General Security Resources	F-4
	F.5.3 General Windows XP Security Resources	F-4
	F.5.4 Specific Windows XP Security Topics	F-5
	F.5.5 Knowledge Base Articles	F-6
	F.5.6 Windows XP SP3-Specific Resources	F-8
F.6	Other Web-Based Resources	F-8

Appendix G— Acronyms and Abbreviations G-1

List of Figures

Figure 2-1. The Facets of Windows XP Security 2-2

Figure 2-2. Typical SOHO Network Architecture 2-11
Figure 2-3. Typical Enterprise Network Architecture 2-12
Figure 2-4. Examples of Specialized Security-Limited Functionality Systems 2-13
Figure 7-1. Disk Management 7-2
Figure 7-2. Folder Options Dialog Boxes 7-3
Figure 7-3. Set Password Dialog Box 7-8
Figure 7-4. File Auditing 7-14

List of Tables

Table 6-1. System Wide Audit Policy Description 6-3
Table 6-2. Additional Registry Values 6-11
Table 7-1. Default User Accounts 7-9
Table 7-2. Default Local Groups 7-9
Table 7-3. Enable TCP/IP Port Filtering 7-22
Table C-1. Certification, Accreditation, and Security Assessments (CA) Family Controls C-1
Table C-2. Planning (PL) Family Controls C-2
Table C-3. Risk Assessment (RA) Family Controls C-2
Table C-4. System and Services Acquisition (SA) Family Controls C-2
Table C-5. Awareness and Training (AT) Family Controls C-3
Table C-6. Configuration Management (CM) Family Controls C-3
Table C-7. Contingency Planning (CP) Family Controls C-4
Table C-8. Incident Response (IR) Family Controls C-4
Table C-9. Maintenance (MA) Family Controls C-4
Table C-10. Media Protection (MP) Family Controls C-5
Table C-11. Personnel Security (PS) Family Controls C-5
Table C-12. Physical and Environmental Protection (PE) Family Controls C-5
Table C-13. System and Information Integrity (SI) Family Controls C-6
Table C-14. Access Control (AC) Family Controls C-7
Table C-15. Audit and Accountability (AU) Family Controls C-8
Table C-16. Identification and Authentication (IA) Family Controls C-9
Table C-17. System and Communications Protection (SC) Family Controls C-10
Table D-1. Commonly Used TCP/IP Ports D-1
Table E-1. Windows XP Tools E-1

Executive Summary

When an IT security configuration checklist (e.g., hardening or lockdown guide) is applied to a system in combination with trained system administrators and a sound and effective security program, a substantial reduction in vulnerability exposure can be achieved. Accordingly, the National Institute of Standards and Technology (NIST) has produced the *Guide to Securing Microsoft Windows XP Systems for IT Professionals: A NIST Security Configuration Checklist* to assist personnel responsible for the administration and security of Windows XP systems. This guide contains information that can be used to secure local Windows XP workstations, mobile computers, and telecommuter systems more effectively in a variety of environments, including small office, home office (SOHO) and managed enterprise environments. The guidance should only be applied throughout an enterprise by trained and experienced system administrators.

The guidance presented in this document is applicable only to Windows XP Professional systems running Service Pack 2 or Service Pack 3. Service Pack 2, which was released in August 2004, contains many changes that may impact security and system and application functionality; accordingly, it is considered a major upgrade to Windows XP. Service Pack 3 was released in May 2008 and causes only minor changes to system functionality and security from Service Pack 2, so security recommendations for systems running Service Pack 2 generally apply to Service Pack 3 systems as well. The recommendations in this guide should not be applied to systems running anything other than Service Pack 2 or 3. Also, NIST has a separate document, Special Publication 800-69: *Guidance for Securing Microsoft Windows XP Home Edition: A NIST Security Configuration Checklist* for securing Windows XP Home systems running Service Pack 2.

This guide provides detailed information about the security of Windows XP, security configuration guidelines for popular applications, and security configuration guidelines for the Windows XP operating system. The guide documents the methods that system administrators can use to implement each security setting recommended. The principal goal of the document is to recommend and explain tested, secure settings for Windows XP workstations with the objective of simplifying the administrative burden of improving the security of Windows XP systems in five types of environments: SOHO, enterprise, and three custom environments, specialized security-limited functionality, legacy, and Federal Desktop Core Configuration (FDCC).

- **SOHO.** SOHO, sometimes called Standalone, describes small, informal computer installations that are used for home or business purposes. SOHO encompasses a variety of small-scale environments and devices, ranging from laptops, mobile devices, and home computers, to telecommuting systems located on broadband networks, to small businesses and small branch offices of a company. Historically, SOHO environments are the least secured and most trusting. Generally, the individuals performing SOHO system administration are not knowledgeable about security. This often results in environments that are less secure than they need to be because the focus is generally on functionality and ease of use.

- **Enterprise.** Enterprise environments, sometimes referred to as Managed environments, are structured in terms of hardware and software configurations and protect their systems from threats on the Internet with firewalls and other network security devices. Enterprise environments generally have a group dedicated to supporting users and providing security. The combination of structure and skilled staff allows better security practices to be implemented during initial system deployment and in ongoing support and maintenance, and for a consistent security posture to be maintained across the enterprise.

- **Specialized Security-Limited Functionality (SSLF).** An SSLF environment is at high risk of attack or data exposure, and therefore security takes precedence over usability. This environment encompasses computers that are usually limited in their functionality to specific specialized purposes. They may contain highly confidential information (e.g., personnel records, medical records, financial information) or perform vital organizational functions (e.g., accounting, payroll processing). Typically, providing sufficiently strong protection for these systems involves a tradeoff between security and functionality based on the premise that any more functionality than is strictly necessary provides more opportunity for exploitation. Thus, a significant reduction in system functionality and a higher risk of applications breaking with increased support cost usually occurs in this environment. An SSLF environment could be a subset of another environment. While some SOHO users understandably might want to choose this environment due to concern for being as secure as possible, this environment is usually not advised for most SOHO users administering their own systems due to the severe tradeoffs and administrative complexity. In most cases, the SSLF environment is also not suitable for widespread enterprise usage.

- **Legacy.** A legacy environment contains older systems or applications that often use older, less secure communication mechanisms. Other machines operating in a legacy environment may need less restrictive security settings so that they can communicate with legacy systems and applications. Using legacy services increases the potential risk of security breaches, as does lowering the security profile of other systems that need to interact with legacy systems. Legacy environments may exist within SOHO and enterprise environments, and in rare cases within specialized security-limited functionality environments as well.

- **Federal Desktop Core Configuration (FDCC).** A Federal Desktop Core Configuration (FDCC) environment contains systems that need to be secured using an OMB-mandated security configuration known as the FDCC. As of fall 2008, FDCC security configurations exist for Microsoft Windows XP Professional Service Pack 2 and Microsoft Windows Vista Enterprise Service Pack 1 systems. FDCC configurations are intended to be deployed primarily to managed systems, so FDCC environments usually have similar characteristics to Enterprise environments.[1]

NIST has provided resources that organizations can use to apply security settings to their systems. For Windows XP systems that are subject to the FDCC mandate, Group Policy Objects (GPO) are available from NIST's FDCC web site (http://fdcc.nist.gov/). For all other Windows XP systems, NIST has made available a set of security templates that will enable system administrators to apply the security recommendations from this guide rapidly. The NIST Windows XP Security Templates are text-based configuration files that specify values for security-relevant system settings. The security templates modify several key policy areas of a Windows XP system, including password policy, account lockout policy, auditing policy, user rights assignment, system security options, event log policy, system service settings, and file permissions. The NIST template for SSLF environments represents the consensus settings from several organizations, including the Defense Information Systems Agency (DISA), Microsoft, NIST, the National Security Agency (NSA), and the United States Air Force (USAF). The other NIST templates are based on Microsoft's templates and recommendations.

By implementing the recommendations described throughout this publication, in addition to the NIST Windows XP security templates or FDCC GPOs and general prescriptive recommendations, organizations should be able to meet the baseline requirements for Windows XP systems. This is based

---

[1] OMB has defined five environments/system roles specific to FDCC. These environments are not directly related to the environments referenced in this publication, and a discussion of the OMB-defined environments/system roles for FDCC is outside the scope of this publication. More information is available from OMB Memorandum 08-22, "Guidance on the Federal Desktop Core Configuration (FDCC)" at http://www.whitehouse.gov/omb/memoranda/fy2008/m08-22.pdf.

upon the management, operational, and technical security controls described in NIST Special Publication (SP) 800-53 Revision 2, *Recommended Security Controls for Federal Information Systems*.

Although the guidance presented in this document has undergone considerable testing, every system and environment is unique, so system administrators should perform their own testing. The development of the NIST Windows XP Security Templates was driven by the need to create more secure Windows XP workstation configurations. Because some settings in the templates may reduce the functionality or usability of the system, caution should be used when applying the baseline security templates. Specific settings in the templates should be modified as needed (with due consideration of the security implications, including the possible need for compensating controls) so that the settings conform to local policies and support required system functionality.[2] NIST strongly recommends that organizations fully test the templates on representative systems before widespread deployment. Some settings may inadvertently interfere with applications, particularly legacy applications that may require a less restrictive security profile.

Windows XP provides multiple ways to deploy templates to systems. The Security Configuration and Analysis Microsoft Management Console (MMC) snap-in can be used to apply a template to a local system, and to compare a template's settings to the existing settings on a system and identify discrepancies. In a domain environment, the Group Policy Editor can be used to distribute security settings quickly from templates to computers in an Active Directory Organizational Unit (OU). Microsoft also offers the Group Policy Management Console (GPMC) for managing Group Policy for multiple domains. GPMC can be used to import, edit, and apply security templates to Windows systems throughout an enterprise, which is ideal for a managed environment.

The security configuration guidance provided in this document was tested on clean Windows XP installations. NIST recommends that system administrators build their systems from a clean formatted state to begin the process of securing Windows XP workstations. NIST also recommends that the installation process be performed on a secure network segment or off the organization's network until the security configuration is completed, all patches are applied, and strong passwords are set for all accounts.

After the Windows XP operating system (OS) has been installed and securely configured, it should be regularly monitored and patched when necessary to mitigate software vulnerabilities as dictated by the patch or software control and change policy and procedures. There are three main methods for updating Windows systems: service packs, hotfixes, and security rollups. The Windows service pack, which provides improvements and replacements to OS components, includes all hotfixes that were released before the service pack cutoff date. Hotfixes are released rapidly when a vulnerability or problem is discovered within Windows systems or Microsoft applications. Security rollups contain several previously released hotfixes in a single bundle. Once Microsoft releases a service pack, security rollup, or hotfix, it should be tested thoroughly and applied to all systems within an organization as soon as possible.

This guidance document also includes recommendations for configuring common Windows applications. The application types include office productivity tools, Web browsers, e-mail clients, personal firewalls, antivirus software, and antispyware software. This list is not intended to be a complete list of applications to install on Windows XP, nor does it imply NIST's endorsement of particular products. Many of the configuration recommendations for the Windows applications focus on deterring viruses, worms, Trojan horses, spyware, and other types of malware. The guide presents recommendations to protect the Windows XP system from malware when the applications are being used.

---

[2] For Windows XP systems that are subject to the FDCC mandate, Federal agencies should use the FDCC baseline and document all changes and other deviations from it.

This document provides recommendations to assist organizations in making their Windows XP systems more secure. The settings and recommendations provide system administrators with the information necessary to modify the settings and to comply with local policy or special situations. The baseline recommendations and settings provide a high level of security for Windows XP Professional systems when used in conjunction with a sound and comprehensive local security policy and other relevant security controls. The guidelines are also appropriate for managed environments that are configuring and deploying laptops for mobile users and desktop computers for telecommuters.

1. Introduction

1.1 Authority

The National Institute of Standards and Technology (NIST) developed this document in furtherance of its statutory responsibilities under the Federal Information Security Management Act (FISMA) of 2002, Public Law 107-347.

NIST is responsible for developing standards and guidelines, including minimum requirements, for providing adequate information security for all agency operations and assets, but such standards and guidelines shall not apply to national security systems. This guideline is consistent with the requirements of the Office of Management and Budget (OMB) Circular A-130, Section 8b(3), "Securing Agency Information Systems," as analyzed in A-130, Appendix IV: Analysis of Key Sections. Supplemental information is provided in A-130, Appendix III.

This guideline has been prepared for use by Federal agencies. It may be used by nongovernmental organizations on a voluntary basis and is not subject to copyright, though attribution is desired.

Nothing in this document should be taken to contradict standards and guidelines made mandatory and binding on Federal agencies by the Secretary of Commerce under statutory authority, nor should these guidelines be interpreted as altering or superseding the existing authorities of the Secretary of Commerce, Director of the OMB, or any other Federal official.

1.2 Purpose and Scope

This publication seeks to assist IT professionals in securing Windows XP workstations, XP mobile computers, and XP computers used by telecommuters within various environments. This guidance should only be applied throughout an enterprise by trained and competent system administrators. Although some of the guidance presented in this document may be applicable to multiple versions of Windows XP, the guidance is specifically intended for Windows XP Professional systems running Service Pack 2 (SP2) or Service Pack 3 (SP3).[3]

The guide provides detailed information about the security features of Windows XP, security configuration guidelines for popular applications, and security configuration guidelines for the Windows XP operating system. The guide documents the methods that IT professionals can use to implement each security setting recommended. The principal goal of the document is to recommend and explain tested, secure settings for Windows XP workstations with the objective of simplifying the administrative burden of improving the security of Windows XP systems in five types of environments: small office/home office (SOHO), enterprise, specialized security-limited functionality (SSLF), legacy, and Federal Desktop Core Configuration (FDCC). The proposed controls are consistent with the minimum security controls for an IT system as represented in the NIST SP 800-53 publication. This guide and its associated templates have been created in support of the NIST National Checklist Program.[4]

---

[3] Released in August 2004, SP2 contains many changes that may impact security and system and application functionality. For more information, see Microsoft's Windows XP SP2 Solution Center (http://support.microsoft.com/ph/6794). SP3 was released in May 2008. More information on SP3 is available from Appendix B.

[4] For more information on the program, see NIST SP 800-70, *Security Configuration Checklists Program for IT Products*, and NIST SP 800-70 Revision 1 (Draft), *National Checklist Program for IT Products*, both available at http://csrc.nist.gov/publications/PubsSPs.html.

1.3 Audience

This document has been created for IT professionals, particularly Windows XP system administrators and information security personnel. The document assumes that the reader has experience installing and administering Windows-based systems in domain or standalone configurations. The document discusses in technical detail various Windows XP security registry and application settings.

1.4 Document Structure

The remainder of this document is organized into eight major sections, followed by seven appendices.

- Section 2 provides insight into the threats and security controls that are relevant for various environments, such as a large enterprise or a home office, and describes the need to document, implement, and test controls, as well as monitor and maintain systems on an ongoing basis.

- Section 3 presents an overview of the security components offered by Windows XP.

- Section 4 provides guidance on installing, backing up, and patching Windows XP systems.

- Section 5 discusses security policy configuration and how security templates can best be used.

- Section 6 provides an overview of the settings in the NIST security templates and explains how the settings can provide better security for systems.

- Section 7 discusses how to apply additional security settings not included in the NIST templates.

- Section 8 makes recommendations for securing office productivity tools, Web browsers, e-mail clients, personal firewalls, antivirus software, and antispyware software.

- Section 9 provides guidance to IT professionals on how to use the guide effectively to secure Windows XP systems.

- Appendix A discusses the NIST security templates and the Federal Desktop Core Configuration (FDCC) Group Policy Objects (GPO).

- Appendix B highlights some of the security changes in Windows XP Service Pack 3 (SP3).

- Appendix C maps the guide's security controls and template settings to the controls in NIST Special Publication 800-53 Revision 2, *Recommended Security Controls for Federal Information Systems*.

- Appendix D lists TCP and UDP ports that are commonly used on Windows XP systems.

- Appendix E lists tools that may be helpful in securing Windows XP systems, and Appendix F lists print and online resources that may be useful Windows XP security references.

- Appendix G lists acronyms and abbreviations used in this document.

IT professionals should read the entire publication, including the appendices, before using the security templates or GPOs or implementing any of the other recommendations or suggestions in the guide. Readers with limited Windows XP administration and security experience are cautioned not to apply the templates, GPOs, or other recommendations to systems on their own. As described in Section 9, effective use of this publication involves extensive planning and testing.

2. Windows XP Security Guide Development

In today's computing environment, the security of all computing resources, from network infrastructure devices to users' desktop computers, is essential. There are many threats to users' computers, ranging from remotely launched network service exploits to malware spread through e-mails, Web sites, and file downloads. Increasing the security of individual computers protects them from these threats and reduces the likelihood that a system will be compromised or that data will be disclosed to unauthorized parties. Effective and well-tested security configurations means that less time and money is spent eradicating malware, restoring systems from backups, and reinstalling operating systems and applications. In addition, having stronger host security increases network security (e.g., home, business, government, the Internet); for example, most distributed denial of service attacks against networks use large numbers of compromised hosts.

The goal of this guide is to provide security configuration guidance to the users and system administrators of Microsoft Windows XP systems. This advice can be adapted to any environment, from individual SOHO installations to large geographically diverse organizations. Although the guide is primarily targeted toward business environments and Windows XP Professional, some of the guidance is also appropriate for other XP versions, such as Windows XP Home, Windows XP Tablet PC Edition, and Windows XP Media Center Edition.[5] This guide draws on a large body of vendor knowledge and government and security community experience gained over many years of securing computer systems.

This section of the guide is based largely on the steps proposed in NIST's FISMA Implementation Project for achieving more secure information systems.[6] Sections 2.1 and 2.2 address the need to categorize information and information systems. Each Windows XP system can be classified as having one of three roles; each system can also be classified according to the potential impact caused by security breaches. Section 2.3 describes threats and provides examples of security controls that can mitigate threats. Section 2.4 outlines the primary types of environments for information systems—Small Office/Home Office (SOHO), Enterprise, Specialized Security-Limited Functionality, Legacy, and Federal Desktop Core Configuration (FDCC)—and ties each environment to typical threat categories and security controls. Section 2.5 provides a brief overview of the implementation of the security controls and the importance of performing functionality and security testing. Finally, Section 2.6 discusses the need to monitor the security controls and maintain the system. Figure 2-1 shows the six facets to Windows XP security that are covered in Sections 2.1 through 2.6.

---

[5] NIST SP 800-69, *Guidance for Securing Microsoft Windows XP Home Edition*, provides step-by-step guidance to Windows XP Home end users on securing their systems. It is available at http://csrc.nist.gov/publications/PubsSPs.html.

[6] More information on the project is available at http://csrc.nist.gov/groups/SMA/fisma/index.html.

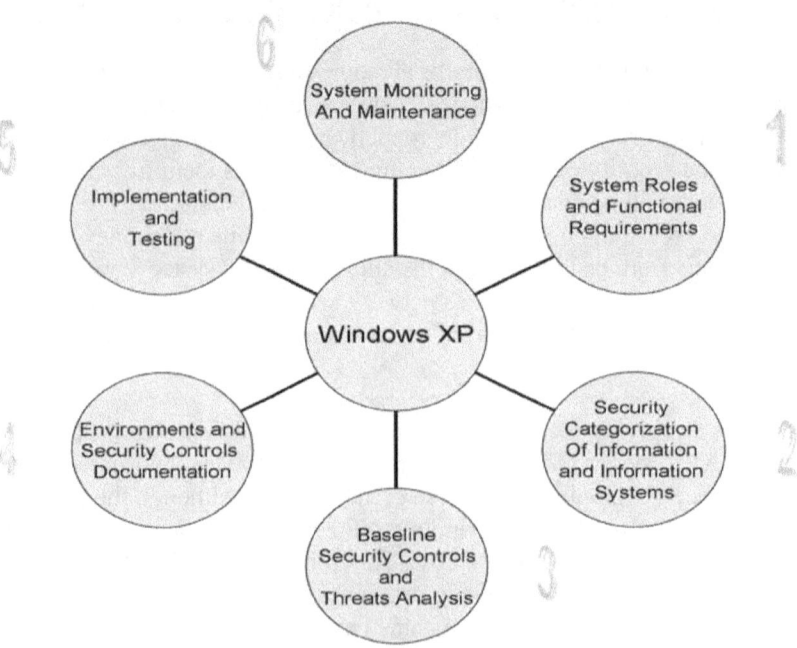

Figure 2-1. The Facets of Windows XP Security

2.1 Windows XP System Roles and Requirements

Windows XP security should take into account the role that the system plays. For the purposes of this guide, Windows XP systems can be divided into three roles: inward-facing, outward-facing, and mobile.

- **Inward-Facing.** An inward-facing XP system is typically a user workstation on the interior of a network that is not directly accessible from the Internet. Physical access is also generally limited in some manner (e.g., only employees have access to the work area). In many environments, inward-facing systems share a common hardware and software configuration because they are centrally deployed and managed (e.g., Microsoft domains, Novell networks). Because an inward-facing system is usually in the same environment all the time (e.g., desktop on the corporate local area network [LAN]), the threats against the system do not change quickly. In general, inward-facing systems are relatively easy to secure, compared to outward-facing and mobile systems.

- **Outward-Facing.** An outward-facing XP system is one that is directly connected to the Internet. The classic example is a home computer that connects to the Internet through dial-up or broadband access. Such a system is susceptible to scans, probes, and attacks launched against it by remote attackers. It typically does not have the layers of protection that an inward-facing system typically has, such as network firewalls and intrusion detection systems. Outward-facing systems are often at high risk of compromise because they have relatively high security needs, yet are typically administered by users with little or no security knowledge. Also, threats against outward-facing systems may change quickly since anyone can attempt to attack them at any time.

- **Mobile.** A system with a mobile role typically moves between a variety of environments and physical locations. For network connectivity, this system might use both traditional wired methods (e.g., Ethernet, dialup) and wireless methods (e.g., IEEE 802.11). The mobility of the system makes it more difficult to manage centrally. It also exposes the system to a wider variety of threat environments; for example, in a single day the system might be in a home environment, an office environment, a wireless network hotspot, and a hotel room. An additional threat is the loss or theft of the system. This could lead to loss of productivity at a minimum, but could also include the disclosure of confidential information or the possible opening of a back door into the organization if remote access is not properly secured.

2.2 Security Categorization of Information and Information Systems

The classic model for information security defines three objectives of security: maintaining confidentiality, integrity, and availability. *Confidentiality* refers to protecting information from being accessed by unauthorized parties. *Integrity* refers to ensuring the authenticity of information—that information is not altered, and that the source of the information is genuine. *Availability* means that information is accessible by authorized users. Each objective addresses a different aspect of providing protection for information.

Determining how strongly a system needs to be protected is based largely on the type of information that the system processes and stores. For example, a system containing medical records probably needs much stronger protection than a computer only used for viewing publicly released documents. This is not to imply that the second system does not need protection; every system needs to be protected, but the level of protection may vary based on the value of the system and its data. To establish a standard for determining the security category of a system, NIST created Federal Information Processing Standards (FIPS) Publication (PUB) 199, *Standards for Security Categorization of Federal Information and Information Systems*.[7] FIPS PUB 199 establishes three security categories—low, moderate, and high—based on the potential impact of a security breach involving a particular system. The FIPS PUB 199 definitions for each category are as follows:

> "The potential impact is **LOW** if the loss of confidentiality, integrity, or availability could be expected to have a **limited** adverse effect on organizational operations, organizational assets, or individuals. A limited adverse effect means that, for example, the loss of confidentiality, integrity, or availability might (i) cause a degradation in mission capability to an extent and duration that the organization is able to perform its primary functions, but the effectiveness of the functions is noticeably reduced; (ii) result in minor damage to organizational assets; (iii) result in minor financial loss; or (iv) result in minor harm to individuals.
>
> The potential impact is **MODERATE** if the loss of confidentiality, integrity, or availability could be expected to have a **serious** adverse effect on organizational operations, organizational assets, or individuals. A serious adverse effect means that, for example, the loss of confidentiality, integrity, or availability might (i) cause a significant degradation in mission capability to an extent and duration that the organization is able to perform its primary functions, but the effectiveness of the functions is significantly reduced; (ii) result in significant damage to organizational assets; (iii) result in significant financial loss; or (iv) result in significant harm to individuals that does not involve loss of life or serious life threatening injuries.
>
> The potential impact is **HIGH** if the loss of confidentiality, integrity, or availability could be expected to have a **severe or catastrophic** adverse effect on organizational operations, organizational assets, or individuals. A severe or catastrophic adverse effect means that,

---

[7] FIPS PUB 199 is available for download from http://csrc.nist.gov/publications/PubsFIPS.html.

for example, the loss of confidentiality, integrity, or availability might (i) cause a severe degradation in or loss of mission capability to an extent and duration that the organization is not able to perform one or more of its primary functions; (ii) result in major damage to organizational assets; (iii) result in major financial loss; or (iv) result in severe or catastrophic harm to individuals involving loss of life or serious life threatening injuries."

Each system should be protected based on the potential impact to the system of a loss of confidentiality, integrity, or availability. Protection measures (otherwise known as *security controls*) tend to fall into two categories. First, security weaknesses in the system need to be resolved. For example, if a system has a known vulnerability that attackers could exploit, the system should be patched so that the vulnerability is removed or mitigated. Second, the system should offer only the required functionality to each authorized user, so that no one can use functions that are not necessary. This principle is known as *least privilege*. Limiting functionality and resolving security weaknesses have a common goal: give attackers as few opportunities as possible to breach a system.

Although each system should ideally be made as secure as possible, this is generally not feasible because the system needs to meet the functional requirements of the system's users. Another common problem with security controls is that they often make systems less convenient or more difficult to use. When usability is an issue, many users will attempt to circumvent security controls; for example, if passwords must be long and complex, users may write them down. Balancing security, functionality, and usability is often a challenge. This guide attempts to strike a proper balance and make recommendations that provide a reasonably secure solution while offering the functionality and usability that users require.

Another fundamental principle endorsed by this guide is using multiple layers of security. For example, a host may be protected from external attack by several controls, including a network-based firewall, a host-based firewall, and OS patching. The motivation for having multiple layers is that if one layer fails or otherwise cannot counteract a certain threat, other layers might prevent the threat from successfully breaching the system. A combination of network-based and host-based controls is generally most effective at providing consistent protection for systems.

NIST SP 800-53 Revision 2, *Recommended Security Controls for Federal Information Systems*, proposes minimum baseline management, operational, and technical security controls for information systems.[8] These controls are to be implemented based on the security categorizations proposed by FIPS 199, as described earlier in this section. This guidance should assist agencies in meeting baseline requirements for Windows XP Professional systems deployed in their environments.

2.3 Baseline Security Controls and Threat Analysis Refinement

To secure a system, it is essential first to define the threats that need to be mitigated. This knowledge of threats is also key to understanding the reasons the various configuration options have been chosen in this guide. Most threats against data and resources are possible because of mistakes—either bugs in operating system and application software that create exploitable vulnerabilities, or errors made by users and administrators. Threats may involve intentional actors (e.g., an attacker who wants to access credit cards on a system) or unintentional actors (e.g., an administrator who forgets to disable user accounts of a terminated employee). Threats can be local, such as a disgruntled employee, or remote, such as an attacker in another country. The following sections describe each major threat category, list possible controls, provide examples of threats, and summarize the potential impact of the threat. The list of threats is not exhaustive; it simply represents the major threat categories that were considered during the selection of the security controls as described in this guide. Organizations should conduct risk

---

[8] NIST SP 800-53 Revision 2, created in response to FISMA, is available at http://csrc.nist.gov/publications/PubsSPs.html.

assessments to identify the specific threats against their systems and determine the effectiveness of existing security controls in counteracting the threats, then perform risk mitigation to decide what additional measures (if any) should be implemented.[9]

2.3.1 Local Threats

Local threats either require physical access to the system or logical access to the system (e.g., an authorized user account). Local threats are grouped into three categories: boot process, unauthorized local access, and privilege escalation.

2.3.1.1 Boot Process

- **Threat:** An unauthorized individual boots a computer from third-party media (e.g., removable drives, Universal Serial Bus [USB] token storage devices). This could permit the attacker to circumvent operating system (OS) security measures and gain unauthorized access to information.

- **Examples:**

    - While traveling, an employee misplaces a laptop, and the party that acquires it tries to see what sensitive data it contains.

    - A disgruntled employee boots a computer off third-party media to circumvent other security controls so the employee can access sensitive files (e.g., confidential data stored locally, local password file).

- **Impact:** Unauthorized parties could cause a loss of confidentiality, integrity, and availability.

- **Possible Controls:**

    - Implement physical security measures (e.g., locked doors, badge access) to restrict access to equipment.[10]

    - Enable a strong and difficult-to-guess password for the Basic Input Output System (BIOS), and configure the BIOS to boot the system from the local hard drive only, assuming that the case containing the OS and data is physically secure. This will help protect the data unless the hard drive is removed from the computer.

    - Secure local files via encryption to prevent access to data in the event the physical media is placed in another computer.

2.3.1.2 Unauthorized Local Access

- **Threat:** An individual who is not permitted to access a system gains local access.

- **Examples:**

---

[9] NIST SP 800-30, *Risk Management Guide for Information Technology Systems*, contains guidance on performing risk assessment and mitigation. It is available for download from http://csrc.nist.gov/publications/PubsSPs.html.

[10] Organizations should have a physical and environmental protection policy that includes requirements for providing adequate physical security for systems and networks. Most technical controls can be easily defeated without physical security.

- A visitor to a company sits down at an unattended computer and logs in by guessing a weak password for a default user account.

- A former employee gains physical access to facilities and uses old credentials to log in and gain access to company resources.

- **Impact:** Because the unauthorized person is masquerading as an authorized user, this could cause a loss of confidentiality and integrity; if the user has administrative rights, this could also cause a loss of availability.

- **Possible Controls:**

  - Require valid username and password authentication before allowing any access to system resources, and enable a password-protected screen saver. These actions help to prevent an attacker from walking up to a computer and immediately gaining access.

  - Enable a logon banner containing a warning of the possible legal consequences of misuse.[11]

  - Implement a password policy to enforce stronger passwords, so that it is more difficult for an attacker to guess passwords.

  - Do not use or reuse a single password across multiple accounts; for example, the password for a personal free e-mail account should not be the same as that used to gain access to the Windows XP host.

  - Establish and enforce a checkout policy for departing employees that includes the immediate disabling of their user accounts.

  - Physically secure removable storage devices and media, such as CD-ROMs, that contain valuable information. An individual who gains access to a workspace may find it easier to take removable media than attempt to get user-level access on a system.

2.3.1.3 Privilege Escalation

- **Threat:** An authorized user with normal user-level rights escalates the account's privileges to gain administrator-level access.

- **Examples:**

  - A user takes advantage of a vulnerability in a service to gain administrator-level privileges and access another user's files.

  - A user guesses the password for an administrator-level account, gains full access to the system, and disables several security controls.

- **Impact:** Because the user is gaining full privileges on the system, this could cause a loss of confidentiality, integrity, and availability.

---

[11] The Department of Justice provides sample banners in Appendix A of *Searching and Seizing Computers and Obtaining Electronic Evidence in Criminal Investigations*, available for download at http://www.cybercrime.gov/s&smanual2002.htm.

■ **Possible Controls:**

- Restrict access to all administrator-level accounts and administrative tools, configuration files, and settings. Use strong, difficult-to-guess passwords for all administrator-level accounts.[12] Do not use the domain administrator accounts from non-administrative client hosts. These actions will make it more difficult for users to escalate their privileges.

- Disable unused local services. Vulnerabilities in these services may permit users to escalate their privileges.

- Install application and OS updates (e.g., hotfixes, service packs, patches). These updates will resolve system vulnerabilities, reducing the number of attack vectors that can be used.

- Encrypt sensitive data. Even administrator-level access would not permit a user to access data in encrypted files.

2.3.2 Remote Threats

Unlike local threats, remote threats do not require physical or logical access to the system. The categories of remote threats described in this section are network services, data disclosure, and malicious payloads.

2.3.2.1 Network Services

■ **Threat:** Remote attackers exploit vulnerable network services on a system. This includes gaining unauthorized access to services and data, and causing a denial of service (DoS) condition.

■ **Examples:**

- A worm searches for systems with an unsecured service listening on a particular port, and then uses the service to gain full control of the system.

- An attacker gains access to a system through a service that did not require authentication.

- An attacker impersonates a user by taking advantage of a weak remote access protocol.

■ **Impact:** Depending on the type of network service that is being exploited, this could cause a loss of confidentiality, integrity, and availability.

■ **Possible Controls:**

- Disable unused services. This provides attackers with fewer chances to breach the system.

- Test and install application and OS updates (e.g., hotfixes, service packs, patches). These updates will resolve system software vulnerabilities, reducing the number of attack vectors that can be used.

- Require strong authentication before allowing access to the service. Implement a password policy to enforce stronger passwords that are harder to guess. Establish and enforce a checkout

---

[12] NIST SP 800-63, *Electronic Authentication Guideline*, contains additional information on password strength. It is available for download from http://csrc.nist.gov/publications/PubsSPs.html.

policy for departing employees that includes the immediate disabling of their user accounts. These actions help to ensure that only authorized users can access each service.

- Do not use weak remote access protocols and applications; instead, use only accepted, industry standard strong protocols (e.g., Internet Protocol Security [IPsec], Secure Shell [SSH], Transport Layer Security [TLS]) for accessing and maintaining systems remotely.

- Use firewalls or packet filters to restrict access to each service to the authorized hosts only. This prevents unauthorized hosts from gaining access to the services and also prevents worms from propagating from one host to other hosts on the network.

- Enable logon banners containing a warning of the possible legal consequences of misuse.

2.3.2.2 Data Disclosure

- **Threat:** A third party intercepts confidential data sent over a network.

- **Examples:**

  - On a nonswitched network, a third party is running a network monitoring utility. When a legitimate user transmits a file in an insecure manner, the third party captures the file and accesses its data.

  - An attacker intercepts usernames and passwords sent in plaintext over a local network segment.

- **Impact:** The interception of data could lead to a loss of confidentiality. If authentication data (e.g., passwords) are intercepted, it could cause a loss of confidentiality and integrity, and possibly a loss of availability, if the intercepted credentials have administrator-level privileges.

- **Possible Controls:**

  - Use switched networks, which make it more difficult to sniff packets.[13]

  - Use a secure user identification and authentication system, such as NT LanManager version 2 (NTLMv2) or Kerberos. Section 3.2.1 contains a discussion of the choices that Windows XP provides.

  - Encrypt network communications or application data through the use of various protocols (e.g., TLS, IPsec, SSH). This protects the data from being accessed by a third party.

2.3.2.3 Malicious Payloads

- **Threat:** Malicious payloads such as viruses, worms, Trojan horses, and active content attack systems through many vectors. End users of the system may accidentally trigger malicious payloads.

- **Examples:**

---

[13] Switched networks cannot completely prevent packet sniffing. For example, techniques such as address resolution protocol (ARP) spoofing can be used to convince a switch to direct traffic to an attacker's machine instead of the intended destination. The attacker's machine can then forward the packets to the legitimate recipient.

- A user visits a Web site and downloads a free game that includes a Trojan horse. When the user installs the game on her computer, the Trojan horse is also installed, which compromises the system.

- A user with administrative-level privileges surfs the Web and accidentally visits a malicious Web site, which successfully infects the user's system.

- A user installs and operates peer-to-peer (P2P) file sharing software to download music files, and the P2P software installs spyware programs onto the system.

- A user opens and executes a payload that was attached to a spam or spoofed message.

■ **Impact:** Malware often gains full administrative-level privileges to the system, or inadvertently crashes the system. Malware may cause a loss of confidentiality, integrity, and availability.

■ **Possible Controls:**

- Operate the system on a daily basis with a limited user account. Only use administrator-level accounts when needed for specific maintenance tasks. Many instances of malware cannot successfully infect a system unless the current user has administrative privileges.

- Educate users on avoiding malware infections, and make them aware of local policy regarding the use of potential transmission methods such as instant messaging (IM) software and P2P file sharing services. Users who are familiar with the techniques for spreading malware should be less likely to infect their systems.

- Use antivirus software and antispyware software as an automated way of preventing most infections and detecting the infections that were not prevented.

- Use e-mail clients that support *spam filtering*—automatically detecting and quarantining messages that are known to be spam or have the same characteristics as typical spam.

- Do not install or use non-approved applications (e.g., P2P, IM) to connect to unknown servers. Educate users regarding the potential impact caused by the use of P2P, IM, and other untrusted software applications.

- Configure server and client software such as e-mail servers and clients, Web proxy servers and clients, and productivity applications to reduce exposure to malware. For example, e-mail servers and clients could be configured to block e-mail attachments with certain file extensions. This should help to reduce the likelihood of infections.

- Configure systems, particularly in specialized security-limited functionality environments, so that the default file associations prevent automatic execution of active content files (e.g., Java, JavaScript, ActiveX).

This section has described various types of local and remote threats that can negatively impact systems. The possible controls listed for the threats are primarily technical, as are the controls discussed throughout this document. However, it is important to further reduce the risks of operating a Windows XP system by also using management and operational controls. Examples of important operational controls are restricting physical access to a system; performing contingency planning;[14] backing up the system, storing the backups in a safe and secure location, and testing the backups regularly; and monitoring Microsoft mailing lists for relevant security bulletins. Management controls could include developing policies regarding Windows XP system security and creating a plan for maintaining Windows XP systems. By selecting and implementing management, operational, and technical controls for Windows XP, organizations can better mitigate the threats that Windows XP systems may face.

Another reason to use multiple types of controls is to provide better security in situations where one or more controls are circumvented or otherwise violated. This may be done not only by attackers, but also by authorized users with no malicious intent. For example, taping a list of passwords to a monitor for convenience may nullify controls designed to prevent unauthorized local access to that system. Establishing a policy against writing down passwords (management control), educating users on the dangers of password exposure (operational control), and performing periodic physical audits to identify posted passwords (operational control) may all be helpful in reducing the risks posed by writing down passwords. Technical controls may be helpful as well, such as using smart cards or another method other than passwords for system authentication.

2.4 Environments and Security Controls Documentation

The section describes the types of environments in which a Windows XP host may be deployed—SOHO, enterprise, and custom—as described in the NIST National Checklist Program.[15] The three typical custom environments for Windows XP are specialized security-limited functionality, which is for systems at high risk of attack or data exposure, with security taking precedence over functionality; legacy, which is intended for situations in which the Windows XP system has special needs that do not fit into the other profiles, such as a requirement for backward compatibility with legacy applications or servers; and Federal Desktop Core Configuration (FDCC), which is for systems that need to be secured using an OMB-mandated security configuration known as the FDCC. Each environment description also summarizes the primary threats and controls that are typically part of the environment. In addition to documenting controls, every environment should have other various security-related documentation, such as acceptable use policies and security awareness materials, that affects configuration and usage of systems and applications. The last part of this section lists some common types of security-related documentation.

2.4.1 SOHO

SOHO, sometimes called standalone, describes small, informal computer installations that are used for home or business purposes. SOHO encompasses a variety of small-scale environments and devices, ranging from laptops, mobile devices, and home computers, to telecommuting systems located on broadband networks, to small businesses and small branch offices of a company. Figure 2-2 shows a typical SOHO network architecture. Historically, SOHO environments are the least secured and most trusting. Generally, the individuals performing SOHO system administration are less knowledgeable about security. This often results in environments that are less secure than they need to be because the focus is generally on functionality and ease of use. A SOHO system might not use any security software (e.g., antivirus software, personal firewall). In some instances, there are no network-based controls such as firewalls, so SOHO systems may be directly exposed to external attacks. Therefore, SOHO environments are frequently targeted for exploitation—not necessarily to acquire information, but more commonly to be used for attacking other computers, or incidentally as collateral damage from the propagation of a worm.

---

[14] For more information regarding contingency planning, refer to NIST SP 800-34, *Contingency Planning Guide for Information Technology Systems*, available at http://csrc.nist.gov/publications/PubsSPs.html.

[15] More information on the program is available at http://checklists.nist.gov/.

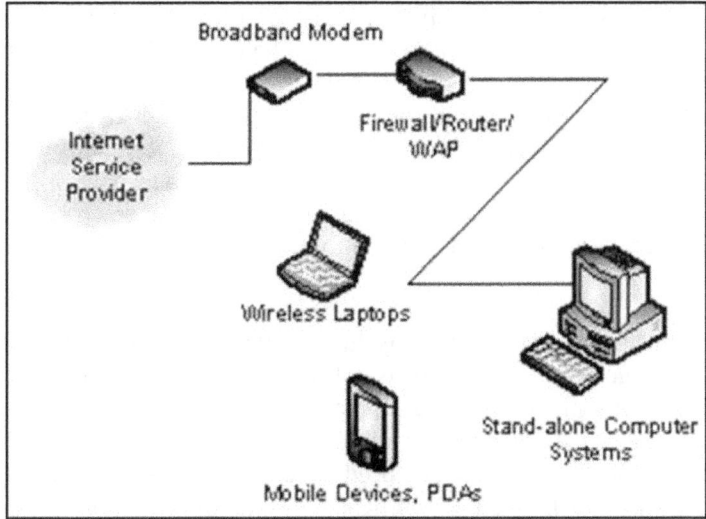

Figure 2-2. Typical SOHO Network Architecture

Because the primary threats in SOHO environments are external, and SOHO computers generally have less restrictive security policies than enterprise or specialized security-limited functionality computers, they tend to be most vulnerable to attacks from remote threat categories. (Although remote threats are the primary concern for SOHO environments, it is still important to protect against other threats.) SOHO systems are typically threatened by attacks against network services and by malicious payloads (e.g., viruses, worms). These attacks are most likely to affect availability (e.g., crashing the system, consuming all network bandwidth, breaking functionality) but may also affect integrity (e.g., infecting data files) and confidentiality (e.g., providing remote access to sensitive data, e-mailing data files to others).

SOHO security is improving with the proliferation of small, inexpensive, hardware-based firewall routers that protect to some degree the SOHO machines behind them. The adoption of personal firewalls is also helping to better secure SOHO environments. Another key to SOHO security is strengthening the hosts on the SOHO network by patching vulnerabilities and altering settings to restrict unneeded functionality.

2.4.2 Enterprise

The enterprise environment, also known as a managed environment, is typically comprised of large organizational systems with defined, organized suites of hardware and software configurations, usually consisting of centrally managed workstations and servers protected from threats on the Internet with firewalls and other network security devices. Figure 2-3 shows a typical enterprise network architecture. Enterprise environments generally have a group dedicated to supporting users and providing security. The combination of structure and skilled staff allows better security practices to be implemented during initial system deployment and in ongoing support and maintenance. Enterprise installations typically use a domain model to effectively manage a variety of settings and allow the sharing of resources (e.g., file servers, printers). The enterprise can enable only the services needed for normal business operations, with other possible avenues of exploit removed or disabled. Authentication, account, and policy management can be administered centrally to maintain a consistent security posture across an organization.

The enterprise environment is more restrictive and provides less functionality than the SOHO environment. Managed environments typically have better control on the flow of various types of traffic, such as filtering traffic based on protocols and ports at the enterprise's connections with external networks. Because of the supported and largely homogeneous nature of the enterprise environment, it is typically easier to use more functionally restrictive settings than it is in SOHO environments. Enterprise environments also tend to implement several layers of defense (e.g., firewalls, antivirus servers, intrusion detection systems, patch management systems, e-mail filtering), which provides greater protection for systems. In many enterprise environments, interoperability with legacy systems may not be a major requirement, further facilitating the use of more restrictive settings. In an enterprise environment, this guide should be used by advanced users and system administrators. The enterprise environment settings correspond to an enterprise security posture that will protect the information in a moderate risk environment.

In the enterprise environment, systems are typically susceptible to local and remote threats. In fact, threats often encompass all the categories of threats defined in Section 2.3. Local attacks, such as unauthorized usage of another user's workstation, most often lead to a loss of confidentiality (e.g., unauthorized access to data) but may also lead to a loss of integrity (e.g., data modification) or availability (e.g., theft of a system). Remote threats may be posed not only by attackers outside the organization, but also by internal users who are attacking other internal systems across the organization's network. Most security breaches caused by remote threats involve malicious payloads sent by external parties, such as viruses and worms acquired via e-mail or infected Web sites. Threats against network services tend to affect a smaller number of systems and may be caused by internal or external parties. Both malicious payloads and network service attacks are most likely to affect availability (e.g., crashing the system, consuming all network bandwidth, breaking functionality) but may also affect integrity (e.g., infecting data files) and confidentiality (e.g., providing remote access to sensitive data). Data disclosure threats tend to come from internal parties who are monitoring traffic on local networks, and they primarily affect confidentiality.

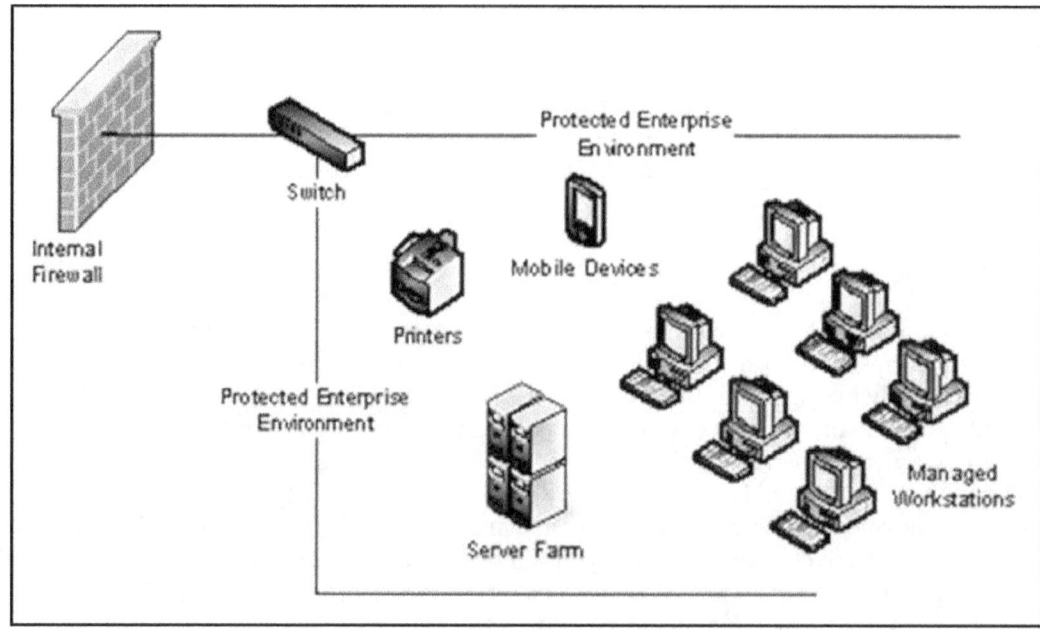

Figure 2-3. Typical Enterprise Network Architecture

2.4.3 Specialized Security-Limited Functionality (SSLF)

A specialized security-limited functionality (SSLF) environment is any environment, networked or standalone, that is at high risk of attack or data exposure. Figure 2-4 shows examples of systems that are often found in SSLF environments, including outward-facing Web, e-mail, and DNS servers, and firewalls. Typically, providing sufficiently strong protection for these systems involves a significant reduction in system functionality. It assumes systems have limited or specialized functionality in a highly threatened environment such as an outward facing firewall or public Web server, or whose data content or mission purpose is of such value that aggressive trade-offs in favor of security outweigh the potential negative consequences to other useful system attributes such as legacy applications or interoperability with other systems. The SSLF environment encompasses computers that contain highly confidential information (e.g., personnel records, medical records, financial information) and perform vital organizational functions (e.g., accounting, payroll processing, air traffic control). These computers might be targeted by third parties for exploitation, but also might be targeted by trusted parties inside the organization.

An SSLF environment could be a subset of a SOHO or enterprise environment. For example, three desktops in an enterprise environment that hold confidential employee data could be thought of as an SSLF environment within an enterprise environment. In addition, a laptop used by a mobile worker might be an SSLF environment within a SOHO environment. An SSLF environment might also be a self-contained environment outside any other environment—for instance, a government security installation dealing in sensitive data.

Systems in SSLF environments face the same threats as systems in enterprise environments. Threats from both insiders and external parties are a concern. Because of the risks and possible consequences of a compromise in an SSLF environment, it usually has the most functionally restrictive and secure configuration. The suggested configuration is complex and provides the greatest protection at the expense of ease of use, functionality, and remote system management. In an SSLF environment, this guide is targeted at experienced security specialists and seasoned system administrators who understand the impact of implementing these strict requirements.

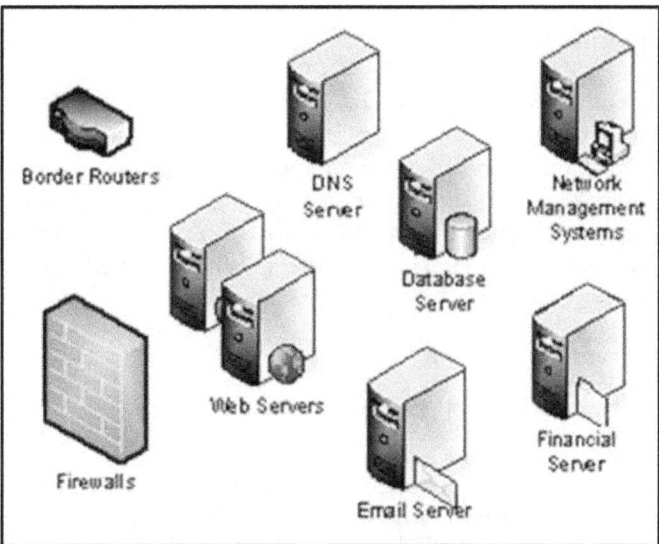

Figure 2-4. Examples of Specialized Security-Limited Functionality Systems

2.4.4 Legacy

A legacy environment contains older systems or applications that use outdated communication mechanisms. This most often occurs when machines operating in a legacy environment need more open security settings so they can communicate to the appropriate resources. For example, a system may need to use services and applications that require insecure authentication mechanisms such as null user sessions or open pipes. Because of these special needs, the system does not fit into any of the standard environments; therefore, it should be classified as a legacy environment system. Legacy environments may exist within SOHO and enterprise environments and in rare cases within SSLF environments as well. Depending on the situation, a legacy environment may face any combination of internal and external threats. The potential impact of the threats should be determined by considering the threats that the system faces (as described in the previous three sections) and then considering what additional risk the system has because of the legacy accommodations.

2.4.5 FDCC

A Federal Desktop Core Configuration (FDCC) environment contains systems that need to be secured using an OMB-mandated security configuration known as the FDCC.[16] As of fall 2008, FDCC security configurations exist for Microsoft Windows XP Professional Service Pack 2 and Microsoft Windows Vista Enterprise Service Pack 1 systems only. The Windows XP FDCC is based on Air Force customization of the SSLF recommendations in this publication and DoD customization of the recommendations in Microsoft's Security Guide for Internet Explorer 7.0. The FDCC configuration is broader than previous configurations for Windows XP, incorporating settings for Internet Explorer, Windows Firewall, and other OS features not included in earlier configuration efforts.[17]

Because the Windows XP FDCC configuration is intended to be deployed primarily to managed systems, the basic characteristics of Enterprise environments, such as primary threats against the systems and baseline technical security practices for the systems, are also basic characteristics of FDCC environments.[18]

More information on FDCC is available in Appendix A.

2.4.6 Security Documentation

An organization typically has many documents related to the security of Windows XP systems. Foremost among the documents is a Windows XP security configuration guide that specifies how Windows XP systems should be configured and secured.[19] As mentioned in Section 2.2, NIST SP 800-53 proposes management, operational, and technical security controls for systems, each of which should have associated documentation. In addition to documenting procedures for implementing and maintaining various controls, every environment should also have other security-related policies and documentation

---

[16] The FDCC home page is located at http://fdcc.nist.gov/.
[17] Although the FDCC configuration includes settings for Internet Explorer and Windows Firewall, it does not mandate their use. Organizations are free to use other Web browser software instead of or in addition to Internet Explorer, and are also free to use other desktop firewall software instead of Windows Firewall.
[18] OMB has defined five environments/system roles specific to FDCC. These environments are not directly related to the environments referenced in this publication, and a discussion of the OMB-defined environments/system roles for FDCC is outside the scope of this publication. More information is available from OMB Memorandum 08-22, "Guidance on the Federal Desktop Core Configuration (FDCC)" at http://www.whitehouse.gov/omb/memoranda/fy2008/m08-22.pdf.
[19] Organizations should verify that their Windows XP security configuration guides are consistent with this publication. Organizations without Windows XP security configuration guides should modify this document to create a configuration guide tailored for their environments.

that affect the configuration, maintenance, and usage of systems and applications. Examples of such documents are as follows:

- Rules of behavior and acceptable use policy

- Configuration management policy, plan, and procedures

- Authorization to connect to the network

- IT contingency plans

- Security awareness and training for end users and administrators.

2.5 Implementation and Testing of Security Controls

Implementing security controls can be a daunting task. As described in Section 2.2, many security controls have a negative impact on system functionality and usability. In some cases, a security control can even have a negative impact on other security controls. For example, installing a patch could inadvertently break another patch, or enabling a firewall could inadvertently block antivirus software from automatically updating its signatures or disrupt patch management software, remote management software and other security and maintenance-related utilities. Therefore, it is important to perform testing for all security controls to determine what impact they have on system security, functionality, and usability, and to take appropriate steps to address any significant issues.

As described in Section 5, NIST has compiled a set of security templates, as well as additional recommendations for security-related configuration changes. The controls proposed in this guide and the NIST Windows XP security templates are consistent with the FISMA controls, as discussed in Section 2.2. The NIST template for SSLF environments represents the consensus settings from several organizations, including DISA, Microsoft, NIST, NSA, and USAF. The NIST templates for the Enterprise, SOHO, and Legacy environments are based on Microsoft's templates and recommendations. NIST has also made available Group Policy Objects (GPO) for the FDCC environment.

Although the guidance presented in this document has undergone considerable testing, every system is unique, so it is certainly possible for certain settings to cause unexpected problems. System administrators should perform their own testing, especially for the applications used by their organizations, to identify any functionality or usability problems before the guidance is deployed throughout organizations.[20] It is also critical to confirm that the desired security settings have been implemented properly and are working as expected. See Section 4.4 for information on tools that can identify security-related misconfigurations and vulnerabilities on Windows XP systems.

2.6 Monitoring and Maintenance

Every system needs to be monitored and maintained on a regular basis so that security issues can be identified and mitigated promptly, reducing the likelihood of a security breach. However, no matter how carefully systems are monitored and maintained, incidents may still occur, so organizations should be prepared to respond to them.[21] Depending on the environment, some preventative actions may be

---

[20] Any changes made to the templates or settings should be documented, as part of the overall documentation of Windows XP systems' security configuration.

[21] Organizations should have an incident response policy and a formal incident response capability. For guidance on incident handling preparation and execution, see NIST SP 800-61 Revision 1, *Computer Security Incident Handling Guide*, available at http://csrc.nist.gov/publications/PubsSPs.html.

partially or fully automated. Guidance on performing various monitoring and maintenance activities is provided in subsequent sections of this document or other NIST publications. Recommended actions include the following:

- Subscribing to and monitoring various vulnerability notification mailing lists (e.g., Microsoft Security Notification Service[22])

- Acquiring and installing software updates (e.g., OS and application patches, antivirus signatures)

- Monitoring event logs to identify problems and suspicious activity

- Providing remote system administration and assistance

- Monitoring changes to OS and software settings

- Protecting and sanitizing media

- Responding promptly to suspected incidents

- Assessing the security posture of the system through vulnerability assessments[23]

- Disabling unneeded user accounts and deleting accounts that have been disabled for some time

- Maintaining system, peripheral, and accessory hardware (periodically and as needed), and logging all hardware maintenance activities.

Organizations should be aware that Microsoft has announced plans to phase out Windows XP and has already stopped selling it. Organizations should consider creating transition plans for an eventual move from Windows XP to a fully supported desktop operating system.[24]

2.7 Summary of Recommendations

- Protect each system based on the potential impact to the system of a loss of confidentiality, integrity, or availability.

- Reduce the opportunities that attackers have to breach a system by resolving security weaknesses and limiting functionality according to the principle of least privilege.

- Select security controls that provide a reasonably secure solution while supporting the functionality and usability that users require.

- Use multiple layers of security so that if one layer fails or otherwise cannot counteract a certain threat, other layers might prevent the threat from successfully breaching the system.

- Conduct risk assessments to identify threats against systems and determine the effectiveness of existing security controls in counteracting the threats. Perform risk mitigation to decide what additional measures (if any) should be implemented.

---

[22] Microsoft offers e-mail alerts that notify subscribers when Microsoft releases an important security bulletin or virus alert. Additional information is available at http://signup.alerts.live.com/brochure/index.jsp.

[23] See NIST SP 800-115, *Technical Guide to Information Security Testing and Assessment*, for more information on performing vulnerability assessments. The publication is available at http://csrc.nist.gov/publications/PubsSPs.html.

[24] http://www.microsoft.com/windows/windows-xp/future.aspx

- Document procedures for implementing and maintaining security controls. Maintain other security-related policies and documentation that affect the configuration, maintenance, and usage of systems and applications, such as acceptable use policy, configuration management policy, and IT contingency plans.

- Test all security controls, including the settings in the NIST security templates, to determine what impact they have on system security, functionality, and usability. Take appropriate steps to address any significant issues before applying the controls to production systems.

- Monitor and maintain systems on a regular basis so that security issues can be identified and mitigated promptly. Actions include acquiring and installing software updates, monitoring event logs, providing remote system administration and assistance, monitoring changes to OS and software settings, protecting and sanitizing media, responding promptly to suspected incidents, performing vulnerability assessments, disabling and deleting unused user accounts, and maintaining hardware.

.

3. Windows XP Security Components Overview

This section presents an overview of the various security features offered by the Windows XP Professional operating system (OS). Many of the components have been inherited from Windows 2000, often with improvements and enhancements. Windows XP also includes several new security features. This guide provides general descriptions of most of these features, with pointers or links to more detailed information whenever possible.

3.1 New Features in Windows XP

Windows XP comes with several new security features. Each new security feature is briefly described below, and most also include a reference to a Microsoft Web page that contains more detailed information. This section also includes an analysis of the security impact of each feature and general recommendations for when the feature should or should not be used. The new security features in Windows XP are as follows:

3.1.1 Networking Features

- **Windows Firewall.**[25] Windows Firewall is a stateful personal firewall.[26] When properly configured, it limits the access that other computers have to the Windows XP machine through the network. This significantly reduces the exposure of the machine to network-based attacks such as the Blaster worm.[27] Windows Firewall can also be used to protect shares when a mobile computer is used outside its normal secure and trusted environment, or to protect access to network shares on an untrusted network. Domain administrators can disable the use of Windows Firewall through Group Policy, but this is generally not recommended unless it is interfering with required functionality or a third party firewall is already in use.[28] Administrators can also use Group Policy to set any Windows Firewall configuration option. Windows Firewall can add another layer to a network security model in enterprise, SSLF, and FDCC environments, and it is sometimes the only layer of network defense in SOHO environments.

- **Network Bridging.** A network bridge allows two dissimilar networks (e.g., Ethernet and dialup, wireless, or token ring) to be joined without using expensive, dedicated hardware. The connection between the two networks is transparent, meaning that no network address translation occurs between the networks and the actual assigned addresses on each network are visible on the other network. While bridging does permit two networks to be joined with a minimal amount of work, it has serious security implications. If a personal firewall such as Windows Firewall is not enabled and configured correctly, the bridge will provide no network security protection to either of the networks that it connects, exposing them to attacks from each other. A network bridge can expose systems on multiple networks to additional threats, so NIST does not recommend implementing a bridge using a Windows XP computer unless it is specifically needed for a task, and risk assessment and mitigation have been performed.

---

[25] Windows Firewall was added to Windows XP in SP2. Before SP2, the built-in firewall was called the Internet Connection Firewall (ICF). For more information on ICF, read Microsoft Knowledge Base (MSKB) article 320855, *Description of the Windows XP Internet Connection Firewall*, available at http://support.microsoft.com/?id=320855.

[26] For more information on Windows Firewall, visit http://www.microsoft.com/windowsxp/using/security/internet/sp2_wfintro.mspx.

[27] The Blaster worm spread by establishing sessions to certain Microsoft TCP service ports (primarily 135, but also 139 and 445). A personal firewall could block unwanted connection attempts to these ports, preventing a worm such as Blaster from successfully infecting a system. For more information on Blaster, see *CERT® Advisory CA-2003-20, W32/Blaster Worm*, available at http://www.cert.org/advisories/CA-2003-20.html.

[28] If interference occurs, NIST recommends that organizations modify the Windows Firewall configuration to permit required functionality, such as internal network vulnerability scans, rather than disabling Windows Firewall.

- **Remote Assistance (RA).** RA provides a way to get remote technical support assistance when running into problems with a computer.[29] RA sessions can be initiated through the Windows Messenger facility, e-mail requests, and via a Web e-mail service (filling out a form to request assistance). Unfortunately, if RA is configured improperly, unauthorized parties could use it to gain remote access to a system. Therefore, RA should be used only if experienced security administrators are available to configure it to strictly limit its usage, and if the network perimeter (e.g., firewall) is configured to prevent external parties from using RA to access internal machines. Otherwise, RA should be disabled.

- **Remote Desktop.** The Remote Desktop feature allows a user to remotely access a Windows XP Professional system from another computer.[30] This provides another method for remote attackers to attempt to gain access to the computer by guessing passwords for default accounts. In general, Remote Desktop should only be used if several other layers of security controls are in place, preventing the system from being directly exposed to attackers. Even then, administrators should carefully consider the business need for having remote access to the system and should think of possible alternatives that will not expose the system to attack.

- **Wireless Auto Configuration**. When a wireless network interface card (NIC) is present, the computer will automatically attempt to join any wireless networks it detects in an established list of preferred networks.[31] This allows a computer to easily roam from access point (AP) to access point without reconfiguration, which is beneficial. However, the system may reveal service set identifier (SSID) information for preferred and previously connected access points, which could be captured by an attacker and used to set up a rogue access point. Because Wireless Auto Configuration can be set to connect to any wireless network, a rogue access point could fool the computer into connecting to a hostile network, which could attack the computer or capture data from it. NIST recommends that systems not be set to attempt to connect to any wireless network automatically.

- **Wireless Security**. To provide a better solution for wireless security, an industry group called the Wi-Fi Alliance has created a product certification called Wi-Fi Protected Access (WPA). In Windows XP SP2 and SP3, hosts with WPA-supporting wireless NICs can use the features provided by WPA, such as using Advanced Encryption Security (AES) for encrypting network communications.[32] Section 7.8 provides recommendations for wireless security, including the use of WPA.

- **TCP/IP Raw Socket Restrictions.** A change introduced in Windows XP SP2 that may impact some users is a restriction on raw sockets for the TCP/IP stack. Some security tools, such as network vulnerability scanners, use raw sockets to craft packets. Windows XP SP2 and SP3 limit the number of incomplete outbound packets per second, which may break such security tools.

3.1.2 Authentication and Authorization

- **Personalized Login.** This feature permits each person who uses a Windows XP computer to have an individual user account, which is recommended. This allows personal data (e.g., each account has its own My Documents folder) and settings (e.g., Internet Explorer bookmarks and security settings) to

---

[29] More information on Remote Assistance, including instructions for disabling it, is available at http://www.microsoft.com/windowsxp/using/helpandsupport/rafaq-general.mspx.

[30] For information on setting up Remote Desktop, read the Microsoft article *Get Started using Remote Desktop with Windows XP Professional*, available at http://www.microsoft.com/windowsxp/using/mobility/getstarted/remoteintro.mspx.

[31] For more information on Wireless Auto Configuration, see the article *The Wireless XP Wireless Zero Configuration Service*, which is available from Microsoft TechNet at http://technet.microsoft.com/en-us/library/bb878124.aspx.

[32] More information on WPA is available at http://www.microsoft.com/windowsxp/using/networking/security/wireless.mspx.

- **Simple File Sharing.**[33] This feature is enabled by default on Windows XP Professional systems in a workgroup, and unavailable on Windows XP Professional systems in a domain. When Simple File Sharing is enabled, only the Guest account can be used to gain access to the system through the network. This means that attackers cannot gain remote access by guessing passwords to other accounts, such as the Administrator account. When Simple File Sharing is not enabled, the administrator can set permissions for different user accounts. Privileges should be restricted so that only those users with a legitimate need to access the system remotely can do so, and so that they have the minimum privileges required.

- **Blank Password Limitations.** In Windows XP Professional, accounts with null or blank passwords can only be used to log on at the physical system's logon screen. This means that accounts with blank or null passwords cannot be used over networks or with the secondary logon service (RunAs). This feature prevents attackers and malware from gaining remote access through blank passwords. Section 6 contains information on other recommended password settings.

- **Credential Management.** Credential Management permits users to store authentication information for operating systems and applications.[34] For example, when a user is prompted to enter a username and password to access a particular application, the prompt window includes a dialog box labeled **Remember my password**. Anyone who gains unauthorized access on that system as the user (e.g., walking up to an unattended workstation) would then be able to use all resources that the stored credentials grant access to. Therefore, passwords should be stored only in environments in which there is a minimal physical threat, or where the password has trivial value (e.g., for a demo on a public Web site).

- **Fast User Switching (FUS).** This feature permits two or more users to be logged into the same Windows XP system simultaneously.[35] Only one user session is active at any given time. The usage of Fast User Switching is recommended on systems where a user may need brief access to a system that someone else is using, because it preserves security and privacy for both users while minimizing the impact on usability. Assuming that each user account has a password, the person currently using the system cannot gain access to the other users' sessions. Fast User Switching is only available on systems that meet certain characteristics, such as those that are not a member of a domain.[36]

- **Distributed Component Object Model (DCOM) and Remote Procedure Call (RPC) Usage.** A feature added by Windows XP SP2 is that anonymous use of DCOM and RPC is no longer permitted. COM servers have access control lists, which can prevent unauthorized access to COM processes. The changes to RPC and DCOM are intended to eliminate several methods used by malware to attack systems. However, these changes may also break many existing programs. All applications that use DCOM or RPC should be thoroughly tested with Windows XP SP2 or SP3 before it is deployed across an enterprise.

---

[33] For more information on Simple File Sharing, see MSKB article 304040, *How to configure file sharing in Windows XP*, available at http://support.microsoft.com/?id=304040.

[34] For an overview of Credential Management, see the Microsoft article *Stored User Names and Passwords overview* at http://technet.microsoft.com/en-us/library/cc786845.aspx.

[35] For a description of how to use Fast User Switching, see MSKB article 279765, *How to Use the Fast User Switching Feature in Windows XP*, available at http://support.microsoft.com/?id=279765.

[36] For more details on this issue, read MSKB article 294739, *A discussion about the availability of the Fast User Switching feature*, available at http://support.microsoft.com/?id=294739.

- **Distributed Transaction Coordinator (DTC) Usage.** DTC is used for handling transactions for databases and other resources. In Windows XP SP2 and SP3, network access by DTC is disabled by default. Windows XP SP2 also adds several security configuration settings for DTC that were not previously available. For example, administrators can specify whether inbound or outbound DTC activity is permitted. Administrators can also require mutual configuration between DTC endpoints, which also causes DTC network communications to be encrypted. Organizations should configure DTC to provide only the access needed by applications and to protect them with mutual authentication and encryption when feasible.

3.1.3 Other

- **Windows Security Center.** Accessible through the Control Panel, the Windows Security Center provides a single interface to various security-related features.[37] It examines the system for firewall software (both the Windows Firewall and third party firewalls). It also attempts to identify installed antivirus software and confirm that it is enabled, configured to perform real-time scanning, and has the most current virus definitions. The Windows Security Center also checks the status of the Automatic Updates feature and makes recommendations on reconfiguring it to ensure that updates are occurring properly. If Windows Security Center detects an issue with a security tool, it will notify the user at login and display a red icon in the taskbar to alert the user of the issue. This should lead to faster identification and resolution of security tool misconfigurations and other problems.

- **Shared Folders.** When enabled, this feature provides folders called Shared Documents and Shared Pictures, which are accessible by all users.[38] This allows users to share files without sharing user accounts or permitting other users to access their personal folders.[39] Shared Folders provide a solution for a SOHO environment for sharing files that any user on the system should be able to access and modify. If more restrictive access is needed (e.g., only certain users, read-only access), the use of Shared Folders is not recommended.

- **Software Restriction Policy.** The software restriction policy allows an administrator to limit what software may be run on a given computer. The software restriction policy can be defined as either restrictive or disallowed. When a restrictive policy is enabled, all programs will be allowed to run except those that are explicitly denied. The disallowed policy will deny the running of all programs except those that have been defined as allowed to run. This can be used to limit the software that can be run to only organizationally approved applications. In turn, this will protect against malware being executed. Although the disallowed policy provides very strong security, it is very time-intensive to set up and maintain, so it is only feasible for certain SSLF environments. The restrictive policy can be useful in preventing the execution of programs with negative security implications, such as peer-to-peer file sharing programs and Trojan horses.

- **Universal Plug and Play (UPnP).** UPnP provides a way for Windows to automatically configure UPnP-aware network devices, such as SOHO firewalls.[40] For example, a Windows XP system could dynamically request that the UPnP-aware firewall open ports to enable a file transfer by an IM client. Windows XP has improved upon UPnP from its original Windows ME implementation, and it now

---

[37] More information on the Windows Security Center is available at http://www.microsoft.com/windowsxp/using/security/internet/sp2_wscintro.mspx.
[38] This feature cannot be enabled unless the filesystem is formatted as NTFS.
[39] More information on Windows XP file sharing is available from MSKB article 304040, *How to configure file sharing in Windows XP*, available at http://support.microsoft.com/?id=304040.
[40] For more information on UPnP, see the Microsoft article titled *Universal Plug and Play in Windows XP*, available at http://technet.microsoft.com/en-us/library/bb457049.aspx.

provides better usability and performance. However, UPnP has had remotely exploitable vulnerabilities, so NIST recommends disabling UPnP unless the dynamic updating feature is needed.

- **Data Execution Prevention (DEP).** Several types of processors include support for Execution Protection (also known as no execute, or NX), which is a way of protecting memory to prevent exploitation. If Windows XP SP2 or SP3 is running on a system that has a processor with NX support, Windows XP's DEP feature can use NX to protect the system from most buffer overflows. Many attackers and malware use buffer overflow attacks to gain unauthorized access to systems or crash them. NX neutralizes buffer overflows by keeping track of which portions of the system's memory contain executable code and which do not. If a buffer overflow attempt causes new executable code to be placed in memory, it will not be run if it is placed in a region that is not marked as containing executable code.[41] By default, DEP is enabled only for essential Windows programs and services when an NX-supporting 32-bit processor is used. On 64-bit processor systems, DEP is enabled for all programs by default. NIST recommends that DEP be configured to protect all programs and services on 32-bit and 64-bit systems, after performing thorough testing to ensure that each program and service does not have incompatibilities with DEP.

3.2 Security Features Inherited from Windows 2000

This section discusses the most significant security features inherited from Windows 2000: Kerberos, smart card support, Internet Connection Sharing, Internet Protocol Security, and Encrypting File System. For each security feature, the section includes a brief description, an analysis of the security impact of each feature, and general recommendations for when the feature should or should not be used. It is outside the scope of this document to cover the features in great depth, so pointers to resources with additional information are provided as needed.

3.2.1 Kerberos

In a domain, Windows XP Professional provides support for MIT Kerberos v.5 authentication, as defined in Internet Engineering Task Force (IETF) Request for Comment (RFC) 1510. The Kerberos protocol is composed of three subprotocols: Authentication Service (AS) Exchange, Ticket-Granting Service (TGS) Exchange, and Client/Server (CS) Exchange. The Kerberos v.5 standard can be used only in pure Windows domain environments.[42] Windows domain members use Kerberos as the default network client/server authentication protocol, replacing the older and less secure NTLM and LanManager (LM) authentication methods. The older methods are still supported to allow legacy Windows clients to authenticate to a Windows domain environment. Windows XP Professional standalone workstations and members of NT domains do not use Kerberos to perform local authentication; they use the traditional NTLM. Because Kerberos provides stronger protection for logon credentials than older authentication methods, it should be used whenever possible. NIST recommends disabling LM and NTLM v1 in SSLF and FDCC environments, and disabling LM in the other environments.

---

[41] More information on data execution prevention in Windows XP is available from part 3 (Memory Protection Technologies) of *Changes to Functionality in Microsoft Windows XP Service Pack 2*, which is located at http://www.microsoft.com/downloads/details.aspx?FamilyID=7bd948d7-b791-40b6-8364-685b84158c78&DisplayLang=en, and from MSKB article 875352, *A detailed description of the Data Execution Prevention (DEP) feature in Windows XP Service Pack 2, Windows XP Tablet PC Edition 2005, and Windows Server 2003*, which is available at http://support.microsoft.com/?id=875352.

[42] For a more detailed explanation of how Kerberos works in a Windows domain environment, refer to MSKB article 217098, *Basic Overview of Kerberos User Authentication Protocol in Windows 2000*, available at http://support.microsoft.com/?id=217098.

3.2.2 Smart Card Support

In the past, interactive logon meant an ability to authenticate a user to a network by using a form of a shared credential, such as a hashed password. Windows XP Professional supports public-key interactive logon by using a X.509 v.3 certificate stored on a smart card. (This can be used only to log on to domain accounts, not local accounts, unless third party software has replaced the built-in graphical identification and authentication [GINA].) Instead of a password, the user types a personal identification number (PIN) to the GINA, and the PIN authenticates the user to the card. This process is fully integrated with the Microsoft implementation of Kerberos. Smart card-based authentication is appropriate for SSLF environments in which strong authentication is required, and one-factor authentication (username and password) is insufficient. Smart cards provide two-factor authentication, because users must possess the physical smart card and must know the PIN. If smart cards or other types of authentication tokens are being used, the organization should have a policy and procedures in place to educate users on properly using tokens (e.g., not sharing them with other users) and protecting them (e.g., immediately reporting a lost or stolen token).

3.2.3 Internet Connection Sharing

Internet Connection Sharing (ICS) allows a Windows XP system to share an Internet connection with other computers.[43] ICS is most often used in SOHO environments (e.g., Internet connectivity provided by a modem on one system). ICS can provide Network Address Translation (NAT) services to the other systems, which essentially hides them from public view. In a corporate environment, domain administrators can prevent systems from using ICS through Group Policy. Portable Windows XP Professional systems do not need to be reconfigured so that they use ICS on a SOHO network but not on a corporate network; Group Policy takes care of it automatically. Generally, ICS should not be used on enterprise networks, but it is a solution for SOHO environments with limited connectivity. It is recommended to use a host-based firewall such as Windows Firewall on the host that is running ICS. Not only can the firewall provide protection for the ICS host, but it can also help to protect the systems behind the ICS from attacks by external parties.

3.2.4 Internet Protocol Security

Windows XP includes an implementation of the IETF Internet Protocol Security (IPsec) standard called Windows IP Security.[44] It provides network-level support for confidentiality and integrity. Confidentiality is achieved by encrypting packets, which prevents unauthorized parties from gaining access to data as it passes over networks. Integrity is supported by calculating a hash for each packet based partially on a secret key shared by the sender and receiver, and sending the hash in the packet. The recipient will recalculate the hash, and if it matches the original hash, then the packet was not altered in transit. Windows IP Security also offers packet filtering capabilities, such as limiting traffic based on the source or destination IP address. Windows IP Security provides a solution for protecting data traversing public networks (e.g., the Internet) and for protecting sensitive data on private networks (e.g., an enterprise LAN). It is also commonly used to protect wireless network communications in enterprise and SOHO environments. Using Windows IP Security in conjunction with a personal firewall such as Windows Firewall can provide protection against network-based attacks by limiting both inbound and outbound packets.

---

[43] For more information on ICS, read the Microsoft article titled *How to configure Internet Connection Sharing in Windows XP*, available at http://support.microsoft.com/?id=306126.

[44] For further information about implementing Windows IP Security, see the *Step-by-Step Guide to Internet Protocol Security (IPSec)* at http://technet.microsoft.com/en-us/library/bb742429.aspx.

3.2.5 Encrypting File System

The Encrypting File System (EFS) provides users a method to transparently encrypt or decrypt files and folders residing on an NTFS-formatted volume.[45] In the original release of Windows XP, EFS could use either the Triple Data Encryption Standard (3DES) algorithm, which is a stronger variant of the Data Encryption Standard (DES), or the Extended Data Encryption Standard (DESX). Windows XP Service Pack 1 (SP1) added support for the Advanced Encryption Standard (AES) algorithm, and SP1, SP2, and SP3 systems use AES by default for EFS. This is a change from Windows 2000, which used DESX by default. In addition, EFS now maintains *encryption persistence*, which means that any file or folder that has been designated as encrypted will remain encrypted when moved to another NTFS-formatted filesystem. Another major change from Windows 2000 is that EFS-encrypted files can now be shared among multiple users over a network.[46] However, files are still transmitted unencrypted across the network (except when Web Distributed Authoring and Versioning [WebDAV] is used, which will transmit encrypted files across networks), so users should transfer the files through a separate encrypting protocol, such as TLS or IPsec. EFS is best used to provide local encryption for files and is particularly useful for laptops and other systems at high risk of physical attack.

3.3 Summary of Recommendations

- Do not implement a network bridge using a Windows XP computer unless it is specifically needed for a task, and risk assessment and mitigation have been performed.

- Enable Remote Assistance only if it is configured so its usage is strictly limited and if the network perimeter is configured to prevent external parties from using it to access internal machines.

- Only use Remote Desktop if several other layers of security controls are in place, preventing the system from being directly exposed to attackers, and administrators have carefully considered the business need for remote access to the system and have not found a viable alternative that will not expose the system to attack.

- Do not configure Wireless Auto Configuration to attempt to connect to any wireless network automatically.

- Only allow users with a legitimate need to access a system remotely.

- Configure systems to store OS and application passwords only in environments in which there is a minimal physical threat or for passwords that have trivial value.

- Disable UPnP unless its dynamic updating feature is needed for compatibility with other devices, such as SOHO firewalls.

- Disable LM and NTLM v1 in SSLF and FDCC environments.

- Use host-based firewalls on systems running ICS.

- As appropriate, use Windows IP Security to protect data traversing public networks and sensitive data on private networks.

---

[45] For more information, see the Microsoft article *Encrypting File System in Windows XP and Windows Server 2003* at http://technet.microsoft.com/en-us/library/bb457065.aspx.

[46] Although multiple users can share EFS-protected files, groups cannot.

4. Installation, Backup, and Patching

This section of the guide contains advice on performing Windows XP installations, and backing up and patching Windows XP systems. It discusses the risks of installing a new system on a network and the factors to consider when partitioning Windows XP hard drives. It also describes various installation techniques and provides pointers to more information on performing them. Another important topic is the ability of Windows XP to back up and restore data and system configuration information. This section also discusses how to update existing systems through Microsoft Update and other means to ensure that they are running the latest service packs and hotfixes. Advice is also presented on identifying missing patches and security misconfigurations on systems.

Organizations should have sound configuration management policies that govern changes made to operating systems and applications, such as applying patches to an operating system or modifying application configuration settings to provide greater security. Configuration management policies should also address the initial installation of the operating system, the installation of each application, and the roles, responsibilities, and processes for performing and documenting system changes caused by upgrades, patches, and other methods of modification.

4.1 Performing a New Installation

This guide assumes that a new Windows XP installation is being performed from scratch. If an administrator or user is upgrading an existing Windows installation, some of the advice in this guide may be inappropriate and could cause problems. Because a machine is unsecured and very vulnerable to exploitation through the network during installation, it is recommended that all installations and initial patching be done with the computer not connected to any network. If a computer must be connected to a network, then it is recommended that the network be isolated and strongly protected (e.g., shielded by a firewall on a trusted network segment) to minimize exposure to any network attacks during installation.[47] If possible, the latest service pack and critical hotfixes should be downloaded from Microsoft's Web site, archived to read-only media, such as CD-ROMs, and kept physically secure.

4.1.1 Partitioning Advice

One of the major decisions during installation is how to partition hard drives. The primary consideration is how large the disk drive is; for example, partitioning is not recommended for drives under 6 gigabytes (GB). For larger drives, the following factors should be considered:

- How large is the drive?

- How many physical drives does the machine have?

- If the system only has one drive, is there a desire to logically separate the OS and applications from data? An example of the benefit of this is that if the OS needs to be upgraded or reinstalled, the data can easily be preserved.

- What is the purpose of this computer? For example, if a computer will be used to share files within a workgroup, it may be useful to have a separate partition for the file share.

- Is there a need for redundancy (e.g., mirroring a data partition onto a second drive)?

---

[47] Installers should follow the organization's policy for connecting information systems or receive direct approval from management before connecting any new Windows XP systems to the organization's networks.

Windows XP Professional provides a feature known as dynamic disks.[48] On a dynamic disk, partition sizes can be changed as needed. For example, an administrator could create an OS and applications partition and a data partition on a large drive, leaving much of the drive space available for future allocation. As needed, the administrator can use the free space to create new partitions and to expand the existing partitions. This provides considerable flexibility for future growth. Users are cautioned that, as with any other new feature, dynamic disks should be tested before deploying them on production systems. Dynamic disks may be incompatible with some applications, particularly system maintenance and management utilities.

Another important consideration during installation is which type of filesystem to use for each partition. NIST recommends using NTFS for each partition unless there is a particular need to use another type of filesystem. Section 7.1 contains more information on NTFS and other filesystem options.

4.1.2 Installation Methods

There are several ways to perform Windows XP installations. This section covers three primary methods: local installations, cloning through Sysprep, and the Remote Installation Services (RIS).

4.1.2.1 Local Installation

The local installation approach refers to traditional methods of installing Windows, such as using a Microsoft CD. This is effective only for installing a small number of computers at a time because it requires user attention throughout the installation. When installing Windows XP from a CD, follow the default steps, except for the following:

- For the Network Setting configuration, select **Custom**[49] and disable all network clients, services, and protocols that are not required. Although this will help to limit the computer's exposure to network-based attacks, consider the implications of disabling each service because this may inadvertently break required functionality (e.g., connecting to remote servers and printers). See Section 7.5 for more information on network clients, services, and protocols. Consider disabling the following services:

    - Client for Microsoft Networks (most users will require this service)

    - Client Service for NetWare

    - File and Printer Sharing for Microsoft Networks

    - QoS Packet Scheduler[50]

    - NWLink IPX/SPX/NetBIOS Compatible Transport Protocol.

- If possible, assign an Internet Protocol (IP) address, default gateway, and domain name system (DNS) server.

- Even if the computer will be joining a domain, choose to be in only a workgroup, and change the workgroup name to something other than the default of WORKGROUP.

---

[48] For more information, see MSKB article 314343, *Basic Storage Versus Dynamic Storage in Windows XP,* available at http://support.microsoft.com/?id=314343.
[49] Throughout this guide, filenames, menu items, and options are indicated through bold text (e.g., **Remember my password**).
[50] QoS stands for Quality of Service.

- Set all environment-specific settings, such as the time zone.

When the installation prompts for accounts to be added, only one account should be added initially. Other accounts can always been added later once the system is fully patched and configured. By default, the account created during the installation and the built-in Administrator account both belong to the Administrators group. After the initial post-installation boot, assign both accounts strong passwords. The next task is to install the latest service pack and hotfixes. Only after the machine has been brought up to current patch levels should it be connected to a regular network. Then, the networking configuration can be changed, such as joining the workstation to a domain, or assigning a workgroup to enable sharing of workgroup resources (e.g., shared directories, printers). Other services that were disabled during installation can be enabled if needed. It is also helpful to scan through the list of installed Windows components, determine which applications and utilities (e.g., Internet games) are not needed, and remove them.

4.1.2.2 Sysprep

Sysprep[51] is a tool that permits an image from a single Windows XP computer installation, known as a *gold system*, to be cloned onto multiple systems in conjunction with a cloning software program such as Ghost or Disk Image. This technique reduces user involvement in the installation process to approximately 5 to 10 minutes at the start of the installation. The Sysprep approach has several benefits. Because the standard image can be created with a strong security configuration, Sysprep reduces the possibility of human error during the installation process. In addition, the Windows XP installation occurs more quickly with Sysprep. This is beneficial not only for building new systems, but also for reinstalling and reconfiguring the operating system and applications much more quickly when needed—for example, as a result of hardware failure or a virus infection. In preparing the "gold" image for Sysprep, the same guidelines used for a local installation should be used, with the addition of enabling any needed services and patching the system. It is also important to physically secure image media so that it is not inadvertently or purposely altered.

4.1.2.3 Remote Installation Services

The Remote Installation Services (RIS)[52] allow a computer to be booted from the network and then to automatically install an instance of Windows XP. RIS can be configured to perform either a completely automated and unattended installation with RISetup, or one that requires minimal user attendance (similar to the Sysprep tool) with RIPrep. Several hardware and software dependencies exist; therefore, Microsoft's documentation on the tool should be consulted for detailed instructions regarding how to configure this installation method.

The RIS method has the same advantages as Sysprep. RIS has the additional advantage of not needing the machine to be installed to have direct access to the physical install media (e.g., a CD-ROM). This can be ideal in an SSLF environment in which machines might not have CD-ROM drives. The primary disadvantage of RIS is that the machine must be connected to a network while it is being installed. This could open up a window of opportunity to exploit a security weakness before installation is completed.

---

[51] Refer to *How to Use Sysprep: An Introduction* at http://technet.microsoft.com/en-us/library/bb457073.aspx for more detailed instructions.

[52] More information on RIS is available from *Remote Installation Services* at http://technet.microsoft.com/en-us/library/cc786442.aspx.

4.2 Backing Up Systems

To increase the availability of data in case of a system failure or data corruption caused by a power failure[53] or other event, Windows XP has built-in capabilities to back up and restore data and systems. By default, users run the Backup or Restore Wizard, which automates most of the backup and restore processes. For example, during a backup the user is presented with several options, including backing up the current user's files and settings, backing up all users' files and settings, and backing up the whole system. This allows the user to back up data and systems without having to manually indicate which files and directories should be backed up, if the user's files are where the backup program expects them to be. To run the Backup or Restore Wizard, perform the following steps:

1. Open **My Computer**. Right-click on the drive that contains the data to be backed up, and select **Properties**.

2. Click on the **Tools** tab. Click on the **Backup Now...** button. This launches the Backup or Restore Wizard.

When a backup is performed, the result is a .bkf file (Backup.bkf by default). If a full system backup is performed, the Automated System Recovery Wizard will prompt the user to insert a floppy disk, which will be turned into a recovery disk that can be used with the .bkf file to restore the system in case of failure.[54] As the name indicates, the Backup or Restore Wizard can also be used to restore a backup from a .bkf file. It is very important to verify periodically that backups and restores can be performed successfully; backing up a system regularly may not be beneficial if the backups are corrupt or the wrong files are being backed up, for example. Organizations should have policies and procedures that address the entire backup and recovery process, as well as the protection and storage of backup media and recovery disks. Because backups may contain sensitive user data as well as system configuration and security information (e.g., passwords), backup media should be properly protected to prevent unauthorized access.[55]

When the Backup or Restore Wizard is run, it presents an option to select Advanced Mode.[56] This switches to the Backup Utility interface, which is not as user-friendly but provides greater customizability and more features. For example, the Backup Utility can be used to schedule backups. In general, system administrators are more likely to use the Backup Utility mode, while end users are more likely to use the Backup or Restore Wizard mode.

Besides the backup wizards and utilities provided by Windows XP, there are also various third-party utilities for backing up and restoring files and systems. It is important to verify that the third-party software can properly back up and restore Windows XP-specific resources, such as the Windows registry and EFS-encrypted files and folders. Windows XP's built-in utilities also use a *shadow copy* backup technique when possible, which means that they essentially take a snapshot of the system and then perform a backup on that snapshot. This avoids problems with attempting to back up open files. Third-

---

[53] An uninterruptible power supply (UPS) and surge protection device can provide temporary emergency battery power when the utility-provided power is unavailable.

[54] For more information on Automated System Recovery, see the Microsoft article titled *How to Set Up and Use Automated System Recovery in Windows XP*, available at http://technet.microsoft.com/en-us/library/bb456980.aspx.

[55] For additional guidance on backups and backup security, see NIST SP 800-34, *Contingency Planning Guide for Information Technology Systems*, available at http://csrc.nist.gov/publications/PubsSPs.html.

[56] For more information on Advanced Mode, see MSKB article 308422, *How to use the Backup utility that is included in Windows XP to back up files and folders*, available at http://support.microsoft.com/?id=308422, and article 309340, *How to use Backup to protect data and restore files and folders on your computer in Windows XP and Windows Vista*, available at http://support.microsoft.com/?id=309340.

party backup utilities used on Windows XP systems should have good mechanisms for handling open files.

4.3 Updating Existing Systems

Host security—securing a given computer—has become increasingly important. As such, it is essential to keep a host up to current patch levels to eliminate known vulnerabilities and weaknesses.[57] In conjunction with antivirus software and a personal firewall, patching goes a long way to securing a host against outside attacks and exploitation. Microsoft provides two mechanisms for distributing security updates: Automatic Updates and Microsoft Update. In smaller environments, either method may be sufficient for keeping systems current with patches. Other environments typically have a software change management control process or a patch management program that tests patches before deploying them; distribution may then occur through local Windows Update Services (WUS) or Windows Server Update Services (WSUS) servers, which provide approved security patches for use by the Automatic Updates feature.[58] This section discusses Automatic Updates and Microsoft Update, as well as patch management considerations for managed environments. This section also defines the types of updates that Microsoft typically provides.

4.3.1 Update Notification

As described later in this section, it is possible to configure Windows XP systems to download critical updates automatically. However, this still leaves other updates that can only be downloaded manually. Therefore, it is important for Windows XP system administrators to be notified of new updates that Microsoft releases. The Microsoft Security Notification Service is a mailing list that notifies subscribers of new security issues and the availability of all types of Microsoft updates.[59] Microsoft security bulletins are also available online from the TechNet Security TechCenter.[60] Individual bulletins are issued for each new vulnerability and are incorporated into monthly bulletins that list the vulnerabilities in order of potential severity (e.g., critical, important, moderate). Each bulletin provides guidance regarding under what circumstances the suggested mitigation strategy (e.g., patch) should be applied.

4.3.2 Microsoft Update Types

Microsoft releases updated code for Windows XP-related security issues through three mechanisms: hotfixes, security rollups, and service packs.

- A *hotfix* is a patch that fixes a specific problem. When a new vulnerability is discovered in Windows XP or a Microsoft application (e.g., Internet Explorer), Microsoft develops a hotfix that will resolve the problem. Hotfixes are released on an individual basis as needed. Hotfixes should be applied as soon as practical for vulnerabilities that are likely to be exploited. (Whenever possible, hotfixes should first be tested on a nonproduction system to ensure that they do not inadvertently break functionality or introduce a new security problem by breaking a previous hotfix.)

- A *security rollup* is a collection of several hotfixes. The security rollup makes the same changes to the system that would be performed if each hotfix were installed separately. However, it is easier to download and install a single security rollup than 10 hotfixes. Microsoft releases security rollups on

---

[57] Organizations should have a configuration management policy that includes requirements for patching systems.
[58] WSUS was released as a replacement for WUS in June 2005. For more information on WSUS, visit the Windows Server Update Services Home site at http://technet.microsoft.com/en-us/wsus/default.aspx. Before Windows XP Service Pack 2, WUS was known as Software Update Services (SUS).
[59] Users can sign up for the notification service at http://www.microsoft.com/technet/security/bulletin/notify.mspx.
[60] The TechNet Security TechCenter is located at http://technet.microsoft.com/en-us/security/default.aspx.

occasion when merited. Security rollups are most useful for updating existing systems that have not been maintained and for patching new systems.

- A *service pack* (SP) is a major upgrade to the operating system that resolves dozens of functional and security problems and often introduces some new features or makes significant configuration changes to systems.[61] Service packs incorporate previously released hotfixes, so once an SP has been applied to a system, there is no need to install the hotfixes that were included in the service pack. Service packs are released every few years; for example, Windows XP was released in the fall of 2001, SP1 in the fall of 2002, SP2 in the summer of 2004, and SP3 in the spring of 2008. Because SPs often make major changes to the operating system, organizations should test the SP thoroughly before deploying it in production. In SOHO environments, the best approach is to delay installation of the SP for at least a few weeks so that early adopters can identify any bugs or issues. However, if the SP provides a fix for a major security issue, and the fix is not available through hotfixes, it may be less risky to install the SP immediately than to let the system remain unpatched.

4.3.3 Automatic Updates

One facility that is available to patch systems with little to no user intervention is the Automatic Updates feature. When enabled, it will automatically check the Microsoft update servers for OS and Microsoft application updates, including service packs, security roll-ups, and hotfixes, as well as updated hardware drivers.[62] Automatic Updates has a prioritization feature that ensures the most critical security updates are installed before less important updates.

Automatic Updates provides three configuration options to users:

- Notifies the user before downloading or installing any updates

- Downloads updates automatically but notifies the user before installing updates

- Downloads all updates and automatically installs them according to a specified schedule.

Generally, it is best to configure the system to download updates automatically, unless bandwidth usage is a concern. For example, downloading patches could adversely affect the functionality of a computer that is connected to the Internet on a slow link. In this case, it would be preferable for Automatic Updates to be configured to notify the user that new patches are available. The user should then make arrangements to download the patch at the next possible time when the computer is not needed for normal functionality. Choosing whether to install updates automatically or prompt the user is dependent upon the situation. If the user is likely to ignore the notifications, then it may be more effective to install the updates on a schedule. If the system is in use at unpredictable days and times, then it may be difficult to set a schedule that will not interfere with system usage. Another issue to consider is that many updates require the system to be rebooted before the update takes effect. Windows XP offers an **Install updates and shutdown** option as part of its Shut Down dialog box, which may be helpful in reminding users to launch the update installation process.

It is highly recommended that the Automatic Updates service be enabled to keep the OS and key Microsoft applications (e.g., Internet Explorer, Outlook Express) fully patched. To enable Automatic Updates, perform the following steps:

---

[61] Additional information on service packs is available from MSKB article 322389, *How to obtain the latest Windows XP service pack*, located at http://support.microsoft.com/?id=322389.

[62] As described later in this section, Automatic Updates can be configured to use a local update server instead of Microsoft's servers.

1. Click the **Start** menu and select **Control Panel**.[63]

2. Double-click **Automatic Updates**.

3. Choose the appropriate radio button (such as **Download updates for me, but let me choose when to install them)**.[64] Click **OK**.

Some organizations do not want the latest updates applied immediately to their Windows systems. For example, in a managed environment it may be undesirable for hotfixes to be deployed to production systems until they have been tested by Windows administrators and security administrators.[65] In addition, in large environments, many systems may need to download the same hotfix simultaneously. This could cause a serious impact on network bandwidth.[66] Organizations with such concerns often establish a local WUS or WSUS update server that contains approved updates and restrict the locations from which updates can be retrieved through group policy. The Automatic Updates feature on Windows XP systems should then be configured to point to the local update server. Unfortunately, although WUS and WSUS provide a method for distributing Microsoft updates, they cannot be used to distribute third party software updates.

4.3.4 Microsoft Update

Users with local administrator privileges can also manually update their systems by visiting the Microsoft Update Web site.[67] The Microsoft Update site will check the computer to determine what security and functionality updates are available and produce a list of updates. The user can then select which updates should be installed at this time, and tell Microsoft Update to perform the installations. To use Microsoft Update, perform the following steps:

1. Run Internet Explorer.

2. From the **Tools** menu, select **Windows Update**.[68] If a prompt appears asking to install and run Windows Update, click **Yes**.

3. If a prompt appears saying that a new version of the Windows Update or Microsoft Update software is available, click on **Install Now** or **Download and Install Now** to install the new version.[69] Multiple updates may be needed. If prompted to do so, close Internet Explorer or

---

[63] Control Panel has two views: Classic and Category. Classic View lists each item separately, and Category View groups similar items together. The instructions in this guide assume that Classic View is being used. To change from Category View to Classic View, click the **Switch to Classic View** link located in the left pane of Control Panel.

[64] These instructions are based on the version of Automatic Updates released in August 2004. The previous version offered the same functionality, but used different wording. On systems with the older Automatic Updates version, select the **Keep my computer up to date** check box, then choose the appropriate radio button (such as **Notify me before downloading any updates and notify me again before installing them on my computer**) and click **OK**.

[65] Some managed environments have software maintenance policies that forbid users from updating systems themselves, primarily because of the possible negative effects of deploying untested updates.

[66] Some organizations deploy updates using read-only media. This is particularly helpful for systems with low network bandwidth (e.g., modems) and systems on untrusted networks (so that they can be patched before being placed onto the network).

[67] Microsoft Update was formerly known as Windows Update. The Microsoft Update Web site is located at http://update.microsoft.com/. The site may only be used with the Internet Explorer Web browser. Windows XP computers that are not fully updated may display the Windows Update Web site instead of the Microsoft Update Web site.

[68] After starting Windows Update, it will display a notification if a new version of the Windows Update software is available, and prompt the user to install the update. To do so, click on **Install Now**.

[69] There are multiple versions of this interface. One states "Get Microsoft Update today!" and waits for the user to click **Go**, then asks the user to click on a **Start Now** button, review a license agreement, and click on **Continue**. After an ActiveX control loads, the user then clicks on **Install** to install the new version of Microsoft Update.

reboot the computer so that the new version of the update software takes effect. (If a reboot is needed, restart these instructions at step 1 after the reboot completes.)

4. Click on the **Custom** button to identify available updates.[70]

5. Microsoft Update checks for updates and lists the available updates. Depending on the service pack level of the computer, either Service Pack 2 or 3 or non-service pack updates should be displayed. Follow the appropriate step:

   a. Non-service pack updates are grouped by high priority updates, optional software updates, and optional hardware updates.[71]

      i. Review the list of available updates, select the desired ones (or accept the default setting), then click **Review and install updates**. In some cases, one patch may need to be installed by itself; therefore, it may not be possible to install all desired patches at once.

      ii. Confirm that the correct updates are listed, and click the **Install Updates** button to perform the installations. Review any licensing agreements that are displayed and click on the appropriate button for each.

      iii. The download and installation process will begin. Depending on the number of updates and the network bandwidth available, it may take from a few minutes to a few hours to download and install the updates. When the installations are done, Microsoft Update should report which updates were successfully installed. It will also prompt the user to reboot the computer if any of the updates require a reboot to complete the installation. Click on **OK** to reboot immediately or **Cancel** to manually reboot the computer later.

   b. Service Pack 2 or 3 can be installed through Microsoft Update using the following steps:[72]

      i. Click on **Download and Install Now**.

      ii. Review the license agreement and click on the appropriate button.

      iii. The service pack should be downloaded and installed. This may take considerable time, depending primarily on the size of the service pack and the type of Internet connectivity and bandwidth available. A setup or installation wizard may prompt the user at some point; click **Next** to continue.

      iv. Once the installation has ended, a summary should be displayed that reports the installation was successful. Click **Restart Now** to reboot the computer.

---

[70] The Custom option can install both high priority and optional updates, and allows the user to select which updates should be installed. The Express option can only install high priority updates, and does not allow the user to specify which updates should be installed. Using the Express option may cause the system to download and install service packs automatically.

[71] High priority updates are defined as critical updates, hotfixes, service packs, and security rollups. Optional updates are hardware and software updates unrelated to security.

[72] If a service pack is being installed from a CD instead of through Microsoft Update, the steps to be performed will differ.

v. After the reboot, the **Help protect your PC** screen appears. The Automatic Updates setting is configured later in the instructions, so at this time, choose the **Not right now** option and click **Next**.

vi. The **Security Center** opens and displays the status of security programs. Since antivirus software and other security programs have not yet been installed on the computer, the current status is irrelevant. Close the **Security Center**.

6. Repeat all of these steps until no more updates are available. Depending on which service pack was on the computer, and the number of additional updates that need to be applied, it may take several rounds of updating the computer and rebooting it to bring a new Windows XP installation completely up to date.

Because Windows Update requires local administrative privileges and is run manually, its use is generally not recommended within enterprise, SSLF, and FDCC environments. As described in Section 4.3.5, it is recommended that all updates be tested and verified before coordinated deployment, which the use of Microsoft Update could circumvent. Microsoft Update has additional complications in enterprise environments because it is typically unrealistic to run any application manually on every workstation in the enterprise on a regular basis, and individual users may not have the necessary local administrative rights.

4.3.5 Patching in Managed Environments

Enterprise, SSLF, and FDCC environments, especially those that are considered managed environments, should have a patch management program that is responsible for acquiring, testing, and verifying each patch, then arranging for its distribution to systems throughout the organization. NIST SP 800-40 version 2.0, *Creating a Patch and Vulnerability Management Program*, provides in-depth advice on establishing patching processes and testing and applying patches.[73] For each patch that is released, the patch management team should research the associated vulnerabilities and prioritize the patch appropriately. It is not uncommon for several patches to be released in a relatively short time, and typically one or two of the patches are much more important to the organization than the others. Each patch should be tested with system configurations that are representative of the organization's systems. Once the team determines that the patch is suitable for deployment, the patch needs to be distributed through automated or manual means for installation on all appropriate systems. (There are several third-party applications available for patch management and distribution, which support many types of platforms and offer functionality that supports enterprise requirements.) Finally, the team needs to check systems periodically to confirm that the patch has been installed on each system, and to take actions to ensure that missing patches are applied.

Microsoft offers the following command-line tools that may be helpful in hotfix deployment, as follows:[74]

■ The **qchain.exe** tool allows multiple hotfixes to be installed at one time, instead of installing a hotfix, rebooting, then installing another hotfix.[75]

■ The **qfecheck.exe** tool can be used to track and verify installed hotfixes.[76]

---

[73] NIST SP 800-40 version 2.0 is available at http://csrc.nist.gov/publications/PubsSPs.html.
[74] The *Guide for Installing and Deploying Updates for Microsoft Windows XP Service Pack 2* is available at http://technet.microsoft.com/en-us/library/bb457071.aspx.
[75] For more information, see MSKB article 296861, *How to install multiple Windows updates or hotfixes with only one reboot*, located at http://support.microsoft.com/?id=296861.

4.4 Identifying Security Issues

Host security is largely dependent upon staying up to date with security patches as well as identifying and remediating other security weaknesses. The Microsoft Baseline Security Analyzer (MBSA) is a utility that can scan the local computer and remote computers to identify security issues.[76] MBSA must have local administrator-level access on each computer that it is scanning. MBSA offers both graphical user interface (GUI) and command-line interfaces. MBSA can identify which updates are missing from the operating system and common Microsoft applications (e.g., Internet Explorer, Media Player, Internet Information Services [IIS], Exchange Server, Structured Query Language [SQL] Server) on each system.[78] For the operating system and a few applications (e.g., Internet Explorer, IIS, SQL Server, Office), it can also identify other security issues, such as insecure configurations and settings. MBSA only identifies the problems; it has no ability to change settings or download and install updates onto systems. The methods discussed in Section 4.3 should be used to download and apply patches.

Enterprise configuration management tools are also available that can be used to assess the security posture of Windows XP systems. These tools have a variety of capabilities, such as comparing security settings with baseline settings and identifying missing patches. Some tools can also correct problems that they find by changing settings, installing patches, and performing other actions. The tools can provide an independent verification that the security controls are implemented as intended and can document this verification for use in demonstrating compliance with laws, regulations, and other security requirements. NIST has been leading the development of the Security Content Automation Protocol (SCAP), which is a set of specifications for expressing security information in standardized ways.[79] Enterprise configuration management tools that support SCAP can use security baselines that are made publicly available by organizations such as NIST, and they can also generate output in standardized forms that can be used by other tools.

Individual systems can also monitor their own security state and alert users of potential problems. Windows XP offers the Windows Security Center, which is a service that can be configured to monitor the state of the system's firewall (either Windows Firewall or a third-party firewall) and antivirus software, as well as the settings for Automatic Updates.[80] Windows Security Center can generate alerts if the firewall, antivirus software, or Automatic Updates feature is not enabled, and also if certain major configuration settings are insecure, such as not setting antivirus software to perform real-time scanning, and not setting Automatic Updates to download and install updates automatically. Windows Security Center can monitor several types of third-party firewall and antivirus software. Windows Security Center is most helpful in SOHO environments, so that users can monitor the security state of their systems. In an enterprise environment, systems might be updated through methods other than Automatic Updates, and the status of systems' firewalls and antivirus software might already be monitored centrally.

---

[76] For more information, see MSKB article 282784, *Qfecheck.exe verifies the installation of Windows 2000 and Windows XP hotfixes*, located at http://support.microsoft.com/?id=282784.

[77] MBSA is available for download from http://technet.microsoft.com/en-us/security/cc184924.aspx.

[78] MBSA cannot identify all types of security issues. Microsoft releases specialized utilities called Enterprise Scan Tools for security issues that MBSA cannot detect, such as patches for Microsoft products that MBSA does not support. More information on Enterprise Scan Tools is available from MSKB article 894193, *How to obtain and use the Enterprise Scan Tool*, which is available at http://support.microsoft.com/?id=894193.

[79] More information on SCAP is available at http://scap.nist.gov/.

[80] For more information on Windows Security Center, see *Manage Your Computer's Security Settings in One Place*, available at http://www.microsoft.com/windowsxp/using/security/internet/sp2_wscintro.mspx.

4.5 Summary of Recommendations

- Use the recommendations presented in this guide only on new Windows XP systems, not systems upgraded from previous versions of Windows. For upgraded systems, some of the advice in this guide may be inappropriate and could cause problems.

- Have sound configuration management policies that govern changes made to operating systems and applications, such as applying patches and modifying configuration settings.

- Until a new system has been fully installed and patched, either keep it disconnected from all networks, or connect it to an isolated, strongly protected network.

- Use NTFS for each hard drive partition unless there is a particular need to use another type of filesystem.

- Disable all network clients, services, and protocols that are not required.

- Assign strong passwords to the built-in administrator account and the user account created during installation.

- Keep systems up to current patch levels to eliminate known vulnerabilities and weaknesses.

- Use MBSA or other similar utilities on a regular basis to identify patch status issues.

5. Overview of the Windows XP Security Policy Configuration and Templates

This section provides an introduction to the concept of Windows XP security templates and describes how the NIST Windows XP security templates were developed. It then provides guidance on how organizations can view, modify, and apply security templates to individual Windows XP systems or to all Windows XP systems within one or more Active Directory Organizational Units (OU). Windows XP also provides a mechanism for comparing the settings in a security template to the current settings on a system; this can be used to identify potential security issues, as well as organization-specific characteristics that may need to be incorporated into the templates.

NIST provides Group Policy Objects (GPO), not templates, for the FDCC specification. See http://fdcc.nist.gov/ for more information on the FDCC GPOs and how to test, modify, and apply them.[81]

5.1 Windows XP Security Templates

In Windows XP, a *security template* is a text-based file that contains values for security-relevant system settings, thus representing a particular security configuration. Templates can be created and updated using the Security Templates Microsoft Management Console (MMC) snap-in. Templates may be applied to a local computer or imported to a Group Policy Object or Group Policy Management Console, which facilitates the rapid deployment of security settings across a Windows XP environment. Templates may also be applied through various commercial change and configuration management tools.[82] The Security Configuration and Analysis MMC snap-in can be used to apply templates to a system and to compare the values within a template to existing settings on a system to analyze the system's security posture.

Windows XP ships with several predefined security templates.[83] Although these templates are included in Windows XP, NIST does not recommend their use. Microsoft intended for the default templates to be used as the basis for creating organizational-specific templates. Several organizations have developed and published their own templates, typically geared toward specific system purposes. Examples include the templates included with the Microsoft Windows XP Security Guide[84] and the templates from the National Security Agency (NSA).[85] As part of the development of this document, NIST has also compiled a set of templates.[86] The NIST template for SSLF environments represents the consensus settings from several organizations, including DISA, Microsoft, NIST, NSA, and the United States Air Force (USAF); the other NIST templates are based on Microsoft's templates and recommendations. They represent the baseline recommended settings advocated by DISA, NSA, NIST, Microsoft, and other security experts. The NIST templates have been customized and fully documented for use on Windows XP workstations in SOHO, enterprise, SSLF, and legacy environments. Use caution when applying any

---

[81] For Windows XP systems that are subject to the FDCC mandate, Federal agencies should use the FDCC baseline and document all changes and other deviations from it.
[82] Examples of change and configuration management tools are Microsoft Systems Management Server (SMS), BindView bv-Control, NetIQ Group Policy Administrator, and Configuresoft Enterprise Configuration Manager (ECM).
[83] The predefined security templates, located in %SystemRoot%/security/templates, are named Setup security.inf, Compatws.inf, Securews.inf, Hisecws.inf, Rootsec.inf, and Notssid.inf. More information on the templates is available from the article *Predefined security templates* at http://technet.microsoft.com/en-us/library/cc787720.aspx.
[84] An overview of the Microsoft Windows XP Security Guide is available at http://technet.microsoft.com/en-us/library/cc163061.aspx.
[85] The NSA's guides and templates for Windows XP are available from http://www.nsa.gov/snac/downloads_winxp.cfm.
[86] The NIST templates are available for download at http://csrc.nist.gov/itsec/guidance_WinXP.html.

of the NIST templates, and if necessary, modify them to conform to local security policy and document all modifications. To view and modify the NIST template settings, perform the following steps:[87]

1. To use the NIST templates supplied with this document, copy them into the **%SystemRoot%\Security\Templates**[88] folder through Explorer.

2. Start the MMC by using the **Start** menu **Run** command, and opening **mmc.exe**.

3. Click on **File**, then **Add/Remove Snap-in**. Click on **Add,** highlight the **Security Templates** snap-in and click on **Add**. Click on **Close**, then click on **OK**. When completed, save the console in the **Administrative Tools** folder for future use.

4. Use the Security Templates snap-in to choose the template that will be applied to the workstation. Navigate through the security template settings and adjust settings as necessary to comply with local security policy. When all changes have been completed, right-click on the template name, choose **Save As**, and specify a new template name. (NIST recommends modifying copies of templates instead of the originals.) The saved template file can then be used on the local computer or other computers in the environment.

5.2 Analysis and Configuration

As mentioned previously, the Security Configuration and Analysis snap-in can be used to compare the current security settings of the local workstation to the settings in a template before the template is applied. This enables system administrators to examine and adjust the changes the security template will make to the computer's settings. To use the Security Configuration and Analysis snap-in to compare and apply security settings on a local Windows XP system, perform the following steps:

1. Start the MMC by using the **Start** menu **Run** command, and opening **mmc.exe**.

2. Click on **File**, then **Add/Remove Snap-in**. Click on **Add,** highlight the **Security Configuration and Analysis** snap-in and click on **Add**. Click on **Close**, then click on **OK**. When completed, save the console in the **Administrative Tools** folder for future use.

3. Create a new database by right-clicking **Security Configuration and Analysis** and selecting **Open Database**. Name the database and click **Open**.

4. Choose the template that will be applied to the workstation. Click **Open** to load the settings from the template.

5. Right-click the **Security Configuration and Analysis** snap-in and choose **Analyze Computer Now**. Specify the default log name and location, then click on **OK**.[89] The system will then compare the current security settings active on the computer with the template settings.

6. When the checks are completed, navigate through the categories of settings listed under the Security Configuration and Analysis snap-in. The differences between the templates and the computer configuration are displayed. For example, items with a red X differ from the template,

---

[87] This method works for all the template settings except for the registry value settings, which are not visible in the MMC. The registry value settings can be adjusted by manually editing the template through a text editor.

[88] %SystemRoot% refers to the Windows directory located on the system drive (i.e., C:\).

[89] By default, the log file is called test.log. The log file records each discrepancy, and may contain hundreds or thousands of entries for a single scan. The same log file is used when a template is applied to the system.

and items with a green checkmark match the template. Other items may not have been analyzed because no setting was defined in the template, or because they were dependent on another value that was not set. Besides the icon, each item also gives a verbal description, such as **Not Analyzed** or **Not Defined**.

7. If a review of the settings indicates that particular template settings should not be applied to the system, they can be adjusted by modifying the database settings shown on the screen. To accomplish this action, double-click on the setting that needs to be altered, make the necessary adjustments, and click on **OK** to return to the main settings listing. Repeat this process until all desired adjustments have been completed.

8. To apply the database settings to the system, right-click on the **Security Configuration and Analysis** snap-in and choose **Configure Computer Now**. Specify the default log name and location, then click on **OK**. The settings are applied to the system.

9. When the configuration is completed, the policy used to apply the configuration can be exported for future use on this computer or others. Export the configuration policy by right clicking on the **Security Configuration and Analysis** snap-in and choosing **Export Template**.[90] Name and save the template for future use on the local computer or other computers in the environment. The saved template file can also be imported to reset settings to a working configuration if future modifications cause problems.

5.3 Group Policy Distribution

In a domain environment, Group Policy Objects (GPO) can be used to distribute security settings to all computers in an Active Directory OU. The recommended method is to separate computers by role into OUs. For example, all similarly configured domain member workstations within an environment should be in an OU. To import a security template into a GPO, perform the following steps:

1. Start the MMC by using the **Start** menu **Run** command, and opening **mmc.exe**.

2. Click on **File**, then **Add/Remove Snap-in**. Click on **Add**, highlight the **Group Policy** snap-in, and click on **Add**. Select the appropriate Group Policy Object and click **OK**, then click **Finish**.

3. Click on **Close**, then click on **OK**.

4. Expand the Group Policy Object. Next, expand **Computer Configuration** and click on **Windows Settings**.

5. Right-click on **Security Settings** and choose **Import Policy**.

6. Select the desired template file and click on **Open**.

The security settings in the template now can be deployed to all computers within the OU. Group Policy can be applied only using a Windows 2000 Server or Windows 2003 Server (domain controller) in a domain environment (Active Directory).[91] Microsoft also offers the Group Policy Management Console

---

[90] If the **Export Template** option is not available, perform the **Analyze Computer Now** step again. The **Export Template** option should then be available.

[91] For more information about Active Directory and Group Policy, refer to http://technet.microsoft.com/en-us/default.aspx and search on Group Policy.

(GPMC) for managing Group Policy for multiple domains.[92] The GPMC combines the functionality of several existing Group Policy-related tools into a single interface.[93] GPMC can be used to import, edit, and apply security templates to Windows systems throughout an enterprise, which is ideal for a managed environment. Once the GPMC has been installed, it can be run simply by executing **gpmc.msc**. To open the GPMC snap-in within the MMC console, perform the following steps:

1. Start the MMC by using the **Start** menu **Run** command, and opening **mmc.exe**.

2. Click on **File**, then **Add/Remove Snap-in**. Click on **Add**, highlight the **Group Policy Management** snap-in, and click on **Add**. Click on **Close**, then click on **OK**.

In GPMC, a GPO needs to be linked to a site, domain, or OU to be used. To link an existing GPO to an OU, perform the following steps:

1. Open GPMC.

2. Right-click on the appropriate OU and select **Link an Existing GPO**.

3. A list of GPOs will be displayed; select the one that should be linked to the OU. This establishes the link.

An alternative is to create a new GPO that is automatically linked to a site, domain, or OU. To create a new GPO for an OU, perform the following steps:

1. Open GPMC.

2. Right-click on the appropriate OU and select **Create and Link a GPO Here**. This opens the New GPO dialog box.

3. Provide a name for the GPO. This creates the GPO and automatically links it to the selected OU.

4. Right-click on the new GPO and select **Edit** to modify the GPO with the Group Policy Editor.

GPMC can import security templates into a GPO. To do so, perform the following steps:

1. Open GPMC.

2. Right-click on the appropriate GPO and click **Edit**.

3. Expand **Computer Configuration** and click on **Windows Settings**.

4. Right-click on **Security Settings** and choose **Import Policy**.

5. Select the desired template file and click on **Open**.

---

[92] More information on the GPMC is available at http://www.microsoft.com/windowsserver2003/gpmc/default.mspx. The GPMC can also be downloaded from this Web site.

[93] For more information on the functionality provided by GPMC, read the Microsoft white paper by Jim Lundy titled *Administering Group Policy with Group Policy Management Console*, available at http://www.microsoft.com/windowsserver2003/gpmc/gpmcwp.mspx.

GPMC can also be used to edit security settings for a GPO. To do so, perform the following steps:

1. Open GPMC.

2. Right-click on the appropriate GPO and click **Edit**.

3. Expand **Computer Configuration** and click on **Windows Settings**.

4. Click on **Security Settings** and then click on the appropriate policy (e.g., Account Policies, Local Policies, Event Log).

5. Modify the security settings as needed and click on **OK** when finished.

Another helpful feature of GPMC is the Group Policy Modeling Wizard, which provides Resultant Set of Policy (RSoP) functionality. This means that the wizard can determine the effects of applying combinations of GPOs (e.g., site, domain, and OU level) to a particular user or computer. To do so for an OU, perform the following steps:

1. Open GPMC.

2. Right-click on the appropriate OU and select **Group Policy Modeling Wizard**.

3. Make the desired selections for the simulation, such as specifying a username, computer name, user location, site, computer location, or security groups.

4. At the **Summary of Selections** screen, review the settings to ensure they are correct and click on **Next** to run the simulation.

5. Once the simulation has ended, the wizard displays the results in a Group Policy Results report. If two or more GPOs had conflicting settings for a particular policy, the report shows which policy was applied. This is very helpful in resolving conflicts among GPOs and troubleshooting unexpected GPO behavior.

Some third-party system management and configuration tools provide similar functionality to GPMC—the ability to import, edit, apply, verify, monitor, and report on security settings in GPOs. These tools may also provide additional functionality, such as in-depth auditing capabilities.

5.4 Administrative Templates

In addition to security templates, Windows XP also supports administrative templates. Administrative templates are used to configure both security and non-security settings (i.e., user interface configuration) for Windows XP and various Microsoft applications. Administrative templates can only be used in association with GPOs, so they cannot be used to secure systems in typical SOHO environments and many legacy environments. Because of that, this publication uses security templates instead of administrative templates.

Administrators of systems in enterprise and SSLF environments may prefer to use administrative templates that include security settings instead of using both administrative templates with non-security settings and separate security templates. Administrators can choose to incorporate the security settings presented in this guide into their administrative templates. Windows XP includes several default administrative templates that address particular types of settings, including general Windows XP settings,

Internet Explorer, Microsoft NetMeeting, Windows Media Player, and Microsoft Update. Administrators could use these templates as a starting point for creating organization or environment-specific templates. Administrators should perform extensive testing of all administrative templates before using them to configure and secure production systems.[94]

5.5 Summary of Recommendations

- Use the NIST security templates or FDCC GPOs to configure security settings on Windows XP systems. Modify the templates and GPOs as necessary to conform to local security policy, and document all modifications.

- Use the Security Templates and Security Configuration and Analysis MMC snap-ins to create, import, view, modify, and export template settings, and to compare template settings with actual system settings.

- Use the Group Policy Object Editor, Group Policy Management Console, and Group Policy Modeling Wizard MMC snap-ins to automate the deployment of security settings to domain member systems.

---

[94] Additional information on administrative templates is available from Chapter 4 of the *Windows XP Security Guide*, which is available at http://www.microsoft.com/technet/security/prodtech/windowsxp/secwinxp/default.mspx.

6. NIST Windows XP Template and GPO Settings Overview

This section provides an overview of the security settings that will be put into place by the NIST templates and FDCC GPOs, as discussed in Appendix A, as well as additional types of settings that can be added to the templates and GPOs. The settings are divided into several categories: Account Policies, Local Policies, Event Log Policies, Restricted Groups, System Services, File Permissions, Registry Permissions, and Registry Values. For each category, this section describes at a high level the related security controls from the templates and GPOs and how the controls can be used to improve the security of the system.[95] This section does not cover all of the actual recommended parameters and values from the security templates and GPOs.

6.1 Account Policies

In addition to educating users regarding the selection and use of good passwords, it is also important to set password parameters so that passwords are sufficiently strong. This reduces the likelihood of an attacker guessing or cracking passwords to gain unauthorized access to the system.[96] As described in Section 3.2.1, NIST recommends the use of NTLM v2 or Kerberos instead of LM or NTLM v1 for authentication. Windows XP offers the same password parameters as Windows 2000. The following parameters are specified in the NIST templates and GPOs:

- **Maximum Password Age.** This forces users to change their passwords regularly. The lower this value is set, the more likely users will be to choose poor passwords that are easier for them to remember (e.g., Mypasswd1, Mypasswd2, Mypasswd3). The higher this value is set, the more likely the password will be compromised and used by unauthorized parties.

- **Minimum Password Age.** This setting requires users to wait for a certain number of days before changing their password again. The setting prevents a user from changing a password when it reaches the maximum age and then immediately changing it back to the previous password. Unfortunately, this setting also prevents users who inadvertently reveal a new password to others from changing it immediately without administrator intervention.

- **Minimum Password Length.** This setting specifies the minimum length of a password in characters. The rationale behind this setting is that longer passwords are more difficult to guess and crack than shorter passwords. The downside is that longer passwords are often more difficult for users to remember. Organizations that want to set a relatively large minimum password length should encourage their users to use passphrases, which may be easier to remember than conventional passwords.

- **Passwords Must Meet Complexity Requirements.** Like the Minimum Password Length setting, this setting makes it more difficult to guess or crack passwords. Enabling this setting implements complexity requirements including not having the user account name in the password and using a mixture of character types, including upper case and lower case letters, digits, and special characters such as punctuation marks.[97]

---

[95] Windows XP SP2 and Windows 2003 SP1 introduce a large number of new Group Policy settings that can be configured with security and administrative templates. For more information on the settings, refer to *Group Policy Settings Reference for Windows Server 2003 with Service Pack 1*, available at http://www.microsoft.com/downloads/details.aspx?FamilyID=7821c32f-da15-438d-8e48-45915cd2bc14&displaylang=en.

[96] Passwords should be protected by other means as well, such as not embedding them within programs and scripts.

[97] These requirements are based on the default password filter (passfilt.dll) included with Windows XP. More information on it is available at http://technet.microsoft.com/en-us/library/bb457114.aspx.

- **Enforce Password History.** This setting determines how many old passwords the system will remember for each account. Users will be prevented from reusing any of the old passwords. For example, if this is set to 24, then the system will not allow users to reuse any of their last 24 passwords. Old passwords may have been compromised, or an attacker may have taken a long time to crack encrypted passwords. Reusing an old password could inadvertently give attackers access to the system.

- **Store Passwords Using Reversible Encryption for All Users in the Domain.** If this setting is enabled, passwords will be stored in a decryptible format, putting them at higher risk of compromise. This setting should be disabled unless it is needed to support a legacy authentication protocol, such as Challenge Handshake Authentication Protocol (CHAP).[98]

Attackers often attempt to gain access to user accounts by guessing passwords. Windows XP can be configured to lock out (disable) an account when too many failed login attempts occur for a single user account in a certain time period. The following account lockout parameters are set in the NIST templates and GPOs:

- **Account Lockout Threshold.** The threshold value specifies the maximum number of failed attempts that can occur before the account is locked out.

- **Account Lockout Duration.** This value specifies how long the user account should be locked out. This is often set to a low but substantial value (e.g., 15 minutes), for two reasons. First, a legitimate user that is accidentally locked out only has to wait 15 minutes to regain access, instead of asking an administrator to unlock the account. Second, an attacker who is guessing passwords using brute force methods will only be able to try a small number of passwords at a time, then wait 15 minutes before trying any more. This greatly reduces the chances that the brute force attack will be successful.

- **Reset Account Lockout Counter After.** This specifies the time period to be used with the lockout threshold value. For example, if the threshold is set to 10 attempts and the duration is set to 15 minutes, then if more than 10 failed login attempts occur with a single user account within a 15-minute period, the account will be disabled.

One of the main challenges in setting account policies is balancing security, functionality, and usability. For example, locking out user accounts after only a few failed logon attempts in a long time period may make it more difficult to gain unauthorized access to accounts by guessing passwords, but may also sharply increase the number of calls to the help desk to unlock accounts accidentally locked by failed attempts from legitimate users. This could also cause more users to write down their passwords or choose easier-to-remember passwords. Organizations should carefully think out such issues before setting Windows XP account policies.

6.2 Local Policies

The Local Policies category encompasses three subcategories: system auditing policy, user rights assignment, and security options. Each of these subcategories is discussed in more depth in the following sections.

---

[98] NIST does not recommend the use of CHAP or MS-CHAP because of known security weaknesses.

6.2.1 Audit Policy

Windows XP includes powerful system auditing capabilities. The purpose of auditing is to record certain types of actions to a log, so that system administrators can review the logs and detect unauthorized activity. Audit logs may also be helpful when investigating a security incident. As shown in Table 6-1, system auditing is available for logon events, account management, directory service access, object access, policy change, privilege use, process tracking, and system events. Each audit policy category can be configured to record successful events, failed events, both successful and failed events, or neither. Section 7.3 describes how file auditing can be configured, as well as how the Event Viewer can be used to review log entries.

Table 6-1. System Wide Audit Policy Description

Audit Policy	Description
Audit account logon events	Audits when a user logs on or off a remote computer from this workstation.
Audit account management	Audits when a user account or group is created, changed, or deleted; a user account is renamed, disabled, or enabled; a password is set or changed.
Audit directory service access	Audits the event of a user accessing an active directory object that has its own System Access Control List (SACL) specified. This setting is not applicable to Windows XP systems.
Audit logon events	Audits users logging on, logging off, or making a network connection to the local computer.
Audit object access	Audits a user accessing an object (for example, a file, folder, registry key, or printer) that has its own SACL specified. Auditing of success or failure of system wide object access will create numerous log entries. Certain object access failures may be normal as a result of applications requesting all access types to objects, even though the application does not require all access types to function properly. Use object access auditing with caution.
Audit policy change	Audits every change to user rights assignment policies, audit policies, and trust policies.
Audit privilege use	Audits each instance of a user exercising a user right. This is likely to generate a very large number of events.
Audit process tracking	Audits detailed tracking information for events such as program activation, process exit, handle duplication, and indirect object access. Enabling this setting will generate many events, so it should only be used when absolutely necessary.
Audit system events	Audits when a user restarts or shuts down the computer or when an event occurs that affects either the system security or the security log.

Recommended settings for system auditing can be applied to systems from the NIST templates and GPOs. Settings can also be applied manually by performing the following steps:

1. From the **Start** menu, choose **Control Panel**.

2. Select **Administrative Tools**, and then choose **Local Security Policy**.

3. Expand **Local Policies**, and then click on **Audit Policy**.

4. The right pane lists the current audit settings. Make any necessary changes by double-clicking on the appropriate item, modifying the setting, and clicking **OK** to save the change.

The NIST templates and GPOs do not enable auditing for specific files or registry keys. Administrators should consider enabling auditing for the most important directories (e.g., %SystemDrive%, directories holding critical user information) and registry keys (e.g., HKLM\Software, HKLM\System). Because enabling auditing for directories and registry keys could cause a large number of auditing events to be generated, administrators should carefully test any such auditing settings before deploying them on production systems.

6.2.2 User Rights Assignment

The NIST security templates and GPOs specify which groups (e.g., Administrators, Users) have certain user rights. The goal is for each group to have only the necessary rights, and for users to only belong to the necessary groups. This is the principle of least privilege, described previously in Section 2.2. Examples of user rights that can be specified are as follows:

- Accessing the system remotely and locally
- Performing backups
- Changing the time and date on the system
- Managing the logs
- Shutting down the system.

6.2.3 Security Options

Besides the Local Security Policy settings mentioned earlier in this section, additional settings called Security Options can be modified to achieve greater security than the default settings provide. The NIST templates and GPOs specify values for dozens of such settings. Examples of the types of settings available are as follows:

- Limiting the use of blank passwords
- Renaming the default Administrator and Guest accounts
- Restricting remote access to floppy and CD-ROM drives
- Encrypting secure channel data in a domain
- Securing the interactive logon screen (e.g., not showing the previous user's account name, displaying a warning banner, prompting users to change passwords before they expire)
- Restricting which types of network access may be performed
- Specifying which types of authentication may be used (e.g., NTLM v2).

The Security Options settings can also be accessed and adjusted manually by performing the following steps:

1. From the **Start** menu, choose **Control Panel**.
2. Select **Administrative Tools**, and then choose **Local Security Policy**.

3. Expand **Local Policies** and select **Security Options**.

4. The right pane lists the security option and indicates the current setting for each. Make any necessary changes by double-clicking on the appropriate security option, modifying the setting, and clicking **OK** to save the change.

6.3 Event Log Policies

Windows XP records information about significant events in three logs: the Application Log, the Security Log, and the System Log. The logs contain error messages, audit information, and other records of activity on the system. The logs can be used not only to identify suspicious and malicious behavior and investigate security incidents, but also to assist in troubleshooting system and application problems. Therefore, it is important to enable logging for all three types of logs. The NIST templates and GPOs enable all three logs for all environments, and also specify the maximum log size. This is important because if the maximum log size is very low, the system will not have much room for storing information on system activity. Some organizations may have a logging policy and central log server, so the template settings may need to be adjusted so they comply with the policy.

6.4 Restricted Groups

NIST recommends that all users be removed from the Remote Desktop Users group on all systems in all environments, except for those users that specifically need to belong to the group. This will reduce the possibility of someone gaining unauthorized access to the system through Remote Desktop. NIST also recommends restricting membership in the Power Users group because it is nearly equivalent in privileges to the Administrators group. Users should not use an account in the Power Users group to operate a system on a daily basis; such accounts should be treated as Administrators group accounts and used only when necessary. Whenever possible, users who need additional privileges, but not full administrative-level access, should be granted the individual privileges needed instead of the range of privileges granted by Power Users group membership. By default, each NIST security template removes all users from the Remote Desktop Users and Power Users groups; the SSLF template also removes all users from the Backup Operators group. The FDCC GPOs do not make any changes to the groups.

6.5 System Services

Windows XP operates with many services that are started automatically when the system boots up.[99] These services consume resources and may introduce vulnerabilities to the host. All unnecessary services should be disabled to reduce the number of attack vectors against the system. In managed environments, the Group Policy Object should be used to configure services on systems; in other environments, services can be shut off individually on each system. For both configuration methods, each service on a system can be configured with one of three startup types:

- ■ **Automatic.** The service is started automatically. This means that the service is running whenever the system is up.

- ■ **Manual.** The service is started only by the system when it is needed. In practice, many services that are reconfigured to Manual are not automatically started when needed; for example, if the Print Spooler is set to Manual, it will not be started when a user tries to print a document. Also, if a service

---

[99] For more information on specific services, see the document titled *Windows Server 2003 System Services Reference*, available at http://www.microsoft.com/technet/prodtechnol/windowsserver2003/techref/sptcgsss.mspx.

is dependent on another service that has been set to Manual, the first service may incorrectly assume the second service is already running.[100]

- **Disabled**. The service cannot be started by the system.

NIST recommends that the following services be disabled in all environments unless there is a specific need that requires them to be enabled:

- Alerter[101]

- ClipBook

- FTP Publishing Service

- IIS Admin Service

- Messenger

- NetMeeting Remote Desktop Sharing

- Routing and Remote Access

- Simple Mail Transfer Protocol (SMTP)

- Simple Network Management Protocol (SNMP) Service

- Simple Network Management Protocol (SNMP) Trap

- Simple Service Discovery Protocol (SSDP) Discovery Service

- Telnet

- World Wide Web Publishing Services.

Each of the NIST security templates disables all of these services; most of them are also disabled by the FDCC GPOs. In addition, the NIST templates and GPOs disable other services such as Computer Browser, Fax, Indexing Service, Remote Desktop Help Session Manager, Terminal Services, and Universal Plug and Play Device Host only for certain environments. It may be challenging, particularly in enterprise environments, to determine which services can be disabled safely. Certain services may be needed only for particular applications. The strategy that best supports functionality is to test each service that appears to be unneeded by setting it to Disabled startup mode and testing all applications.

---

[100] Because of these issues, NIST recommends setting a service's startup type to Manual only if Manual is the default startup type for the service.

[101] Windows XP SP2 and SP3 disable the Alerter and Messenger services by default. These services are intended to be used to display alerts and information. For example, an administrator could send a message to all users' screens, notifying them that a particular server is being taken down for maintenance. Unfortunately, these services have been misused by attackers and spammers to generate messages on users' screens. A description of this issue is available at http://support.microsoft.com/?id=330904. Windows Firewall restricts some of the Messenger ports by default so that they only accept packets with source addresses on the local subnet, which may help to alleviate the misuse issues if the services are needed for administrative purposes in an enterprise environment.

To change the startup mode for a particular service, perform the following steps:

1. Click the **Start** menu and choose **Control Panel**.

2. Select **Administrative Tools** and then select **Services**.

3. Click the **Standard** tab view located at the bottom of the window.

4. Double-click the service name (e.g., ClipBook).

5. If the service should be set to Manual or Disabled, click the **Stop** button if the service is started.

6. Set the Startup type to **Automatic**, **Manual**, or **Disabled** and click **OK**.

7. Exit the **Computer Management** tool.

To disable the Universal Plug and Play feature, follow the steps above for both the SSDP Discovery Service and the Universal Plug and Play (UPnP) Device Host service.

The procedure for disabling the Remote Assistance and Remote Desktop features is different than disabling other services. Although these features are helpful for support, they also expose the computer to network-based attacks. As such, unless an organizational requirement exists to have them enabled, perform the following steps to disable them:

1. Right-click **My Computer** and select **Properties**.

2. Select the **Remote** tab and uncheck the **Allow Remote Assistance invitations to be sent from this computer** and **Allow users to connect remotely to this computer** boxes. Click **OK**.

6.6 File Permissions

This section provides general instructions regarding setting permissions through file system access control entries (ACE)[102] and access control lists (ACL) for Windows XP.[103] The NIST templates and GPOs restrict access to dozens of executables, protecting them from unauthorized modification and usage. Additional custom settings may be added that are specific to the environment in which the Windows XP machine resides. Changes to an ACL for a specific resource, such as a file or folder, can be made using one of three possible methods:

- Open the **Properties** window for a resource from its context menu and click on the **Security** tab. It displays the privileges that each user or group has to the resource. The **Advanced** button can be used to set more granular permission rights and additional settings such as file auditing and the owner of the resource.

---

[102] An ACE is an entry that binds a security identifier (SID) to a set of permissions within an ACL.
[103] Once file permissions are applied, there is not an automatic way to undo them or otherwise return the files to their previous permissions. Additional procedures, such as recording the original file permissions before applying new ones, may be needed to provide an undo capability. The same is true for the registry permissions described in Section 6.7.

- Use the utility **cacls.exe** found in **%SystemRoot%\system32**.[104] This is a command-line interface used to set file ACLs, but it does not set Windows XP security descriptors.

- Use the **MMC Security Template** snap-in to apply settings from a template.

Windows XP uses an inheritance model for assigning ACEs. An object's ACL can contain ACEs that it inherited from its parent container. For example, a file in an NTFS filesystem can inherit ACEs from the directory that contains it. In addition, an ACE that is directly applied to a filesystem object is given a higher priority than an inherited ACE. The directly applied ACE overrides any conflicting inherited ACEs.

6.7 Registry Permissions

Windows XP also has permissions for the registry. The NIST templates and GPOs do not contain any registry permissions, but administrators should set restrictive permissions for several registry keys and values to protect them from unauthorized access and modifications. Changing registry permissions can negatively impact the functionality and stability of Windows XP systems, so administrators should carefully test any such permissions before deploying them on production systems.

By default, permission to manipulate the registry is restricted, but because of the value of the registry, it is important to verify that the registry is protected. To do so, perform the following steps:

1. Click **Start** and select **Run**. Type **regedit** and click **OK**.

2. Locate the key **HKEY_LOCAL_MACHINE\SYSTEM\CurrentControlSet\Control\SecurePipeServers\winreg**.

3. Right-click on **winreg** and select **Permissions**. Ensure that only the **Administrator** has **Full Control,** the **Backup Operators** group has no permissions (other than the special permissions Query Value, Enumerate Subkeys, Notify, and Read Control), and **LOCAL SERVICE** has only **Read** permissions.

6.8 Registry Values

The NIST templates set values for several registry keys not previously mentioned in this section. The following items provide the registry key name and path, describe its purpose, and recommend an appropriate setting.[105]

6.8.1 Automatic Functions

- **HKLM\Software\Microsoft\Windows\CurrentVersion\Policies\Explorer\NoDriveTypeAutoRun.**[106] The autorun feature attempts to run content from a CD automatically when it is placed in the system. If a CD contains malicious content, it could be automatically run. Setting this registry value to 255 disables the autorun feature for all types of drives.

---

[104] **%SystemDrive%** refers to the actual partition or hard drive in which Windows XP is installed, typically the **C:** drive. **%SystemRoot%** refers to the folder on **%SystemDrive%** where Windows XP files are installed, typically the **Windows** directory.

[105] Some of these settings may not appear in the Group Policy Editor. See http://blogs.technet.com/fdcc/archive/2008/01/29/why-don-t-all-of-the-fdcc-settings-appear-in-the-group-policy-editor.aspx for additional information.

[106] HKLM is an abbreviation for HKEY_LOCAL_MACHINE.

- **HKLM\Software\Microsoft\Windows NT\CurrentVersion\Winlogon\AutoAdminLogon.** If enabled, this registry value allows the system login to be bypassed by using a password stored in cleartext within the registry. This password may be viewable by local users of the system. Also, an unauthorized party who gains physical access to the system may be able to gain access without providing any authentication. Setting the registry value to 0 disables the feature.

6.8.2 Networking

The settings described in this section modify Microsoft TCP/IP stack settings and other aspects of Windows XP networking.

- **HKLM\System\CurrentControlSet\Services\IPSec\NoDefaultExempt.** In Windows XP, IPsec has certain default exemptions to its policy filters. This parameter should usually be set to 1, which removes the exemptions for Kerberos and RSVP traffic.[107]

- **HKLM\System\CurrentControlSet\Services\LanManServer\Parameters\AutoShareWks.** If the File and Printer Sharing for Microsoft Networks service is being used, Windows XP will share all local fixed drives as hidden administrative resources (e.g., C$, D$). It is recommended that these shares be disabled unless they are necessary. For example, some software applications may rely on the existence of one of the shares. In addition, in environments in which systems are maintained remotely, the shares may be needed to facilitate the maintenance process. If the shares are not needed, setting this registry value to 0 will suppress them.

- **HKLM\System\CurrentControlSet\Services\LanManServer\Parameters\Hidden.** Setting this parameter to 1 prevents the system's Server service from sending out browser announcements, which causes the system to be hidden from the Browser on other systems. This reduces the likelihood that other users on the network will attempt to gain access to the system through Microsoft networking.

- **HKLM\System\CurrentControlSet\Services\Tcpip\Parameters\DisableIPSourceRouting.** Setting this parameter to 2 will disable IP packet source routing. Source routing generally has no legitimate purpose and can be used by attackers to redirect packets through a particular intermediate host. This could allow an attacker to view and modify network communications.

- **HKLM\System\CurrentControlSet\Services\Tcpip\Parameters\EnableDeadGWDetect.** When this value is set to 1, TCP is allowed to perform dead gateway detection. With this feature enabled, TCP may ask IP to change to a backup gateway if a number of connections are experiencing difficulty. An attacker could take advantage of this to trick the system into using a malicious gateway, which could allow the attacker to view and modify data, or to cause a denial of service. Setting this parameter to 0 disables the dead gateway detection feature.

- **HKLM\System\CurrentControlSet\Services\Tcpip\Parameters\EnableICMPRedirect.** If this feature is enabled, Windows XP will alter its routing table in response to ICMP redirect messages that are sent to it by network devices such as routers. Attackers can spoof ICMP redirect messages to trick systems into routing packets to the attacker's system (or elsewhere), which could permit a third party to intercept sensitive information, breach the system, or cause a denial of service. Setting the registry value to 0 disables this feature.

- **HKLM\System\CurrentControlSet\Services\Tcpip\Parameters\KeepAliveTime.** This is a parameter that controls how often TCP attempts to verify that an idle connection is still intact by

---

[107] For more information on this parameter, see MSKB article 810207, *IPSec default exemptions are removed in Windows Server 2003*, available at http://support.microsoft.com/?id=810207.

sending a keep-alive packet. If the remote system is still reachable and functioning, it acknowledges the keep-alive transmission. Keep-alive packets are not sent by default. This feature may be enabled for a connection by an application. The NIST SSLF template sets the keep-alive time to 300,000 milliseconds (5 minutes).

- **HKLM\System\CurrentControlSet\Services\Netbt\Parameters\NoNameReleaseOnDemand.** This parameter determines whether the computer releases its NetBIOS name when it receives a name-release request from the network. Setting this to 1 prevents the system from releasing its name, which can protect the system from malicious name-release attacks, but might also impair normal operations.

- **HKLM\System\CurrentControlSet\Services\Tcpip\Parameters\SynAttackProtect.** This feature enables protection against synflood attacks. If the TcpMaxHalfOpen and TcpMaxHalfOpenRetried registry values have been set appropriately, this feature reduces retransmission retries and delayed route cache entry (RCE) creation. Setting this parameter to 1 or 2 enables synflood attack protection; 2 provides more robust protection than setting it to 1.

- **HKLM\System\CurrentControlSet\Services\Tcpip\Parameters\TcpMaxConnectResponseRetransmissions.** This sets how many times TCP will retransmit a SYN-ACK packet that has not been acknowledged.

- **HKLM\System\CurrentControlSet\Services\Tcpip\Parameters\TcpMaxDataRetransmissions.** This sets how many times TCP will retransmit a packet that has not been acknowledged from a fully established connection.

6.8.3 Other Template Settings

These settings correspond to other registry keys set in the templates that do not fit into the categories in Sections 6.8.1 and 6.8.2.

- **HKLM\Software\Microsoft\Windows NT\CurrentVersion\Winlogon\ScreenSaverGracePeriod.** This value sets the grace period between the activation of a password-protected screen saver and the requirement to enter a password to unlock the system. Setting this value to 0 eliminates the grace period.

- **HKLM\System\CurrentControlSet\Control\FileSystem\NtfsDisable8dot3NameCreation.** Setting this value to 1 disables the automatic creation of legacy filenames in 8.3 format.

- **HKLM\System\CurrentControlSet\Control\Session Manager\SafeDllSearchMode.** Windows XP searches directories in a particular order when it is looking for a file to execute. By default, Windows searches the current directory before the Windows and system directories. Setting this parameter to 1 causes Windows to search the Windows and system directories before searching the current directory. This is a better security practice because the current directory may be less restrictive than the Windows and system directories. For example, a malicious user on a system could place a Trojan horse in a shared directory. If the default search order is used, another user who attempts to run a program with the same name could inadvertently run the Trojan horse instead. If the suggested search order is used, the Trojan horse would not be run.

- **HKLM\System\CurrentControlSet\Services\EventLog\Security\WarningLevel.** This value corresponds to a percentage of the maximum size of the security event log. When the security event log's size reaches the specified percentage, the system issues a warning.

- **HKLM\System\CurrentControlSet\Services\RasMan\Parameters\DisableSavePassword.**
  Setting this parameter to 1 prevents the Network Connections phone book from saving passwords used for remote access.

6.8.4 Settings Not In the NIST Templates

Table 6-2 lists additional registry values related to security that are not defined in the NIST templates.

Table 6-2. Additional Registry Values[108]

Item	Registry Value Name and Path	Recommended Data Value[109]	Explanation
1	HKLM\Software\Microsoft\DrWatson\CreateCrashDump	0	Setting this value to 0 disables the creation of a memory dump file by the Dr. Watson program debugger. Memory dumps can contain sensitive information such as passwords. See Section 7.9 for additional information on suppressing memory dump file creation. This setting should be enabled to troubleshoot a recurring problem.
2	HKLM\Software\Microsoft \Windows NT\CurrentVersion\AEDebug\Auto	0	Setting this value to 0 disables Dr. Watson.
3	HKLM\System\CurrentControlSet\Services\CDrom\Autorun	0	Setting this value to 0 disables the autorun feature for CDs.
4	HKLM\System\CurrentControlSet\Services\MrxSmb\Parameters\RefuseReset	Not defined	Setting this parameter to 1 causes the system to ignore ResetBrowser frames. Such frames can be used to shut down NetBIOS and master browsers and to declare a computer as being the new master browser. Earlier versions of Windows could be attacked through ResetBrowser frames.
5	HKLM\System\CurrentControlSet\Services\Tcpip\Parameters\EnablePMTUDiscovery	Not defined	When this parameter is set to 1, TCP attempts to discover the Maximum Transmission Unit (MTU), the size of the largest packet that can be kept intact over the path to a remote host. Setting this parameter to 0 disables the feature and causes an MTU of 576 bytes to be used for all connections that are not made to hosts on the local subnet.
6	HKLM\System\CurrentControlSet\Services\Tcpip\Parameters\PerformRouterDiscovery	0	This parameter controls whether the system attempts to perform router discovery per RFC 1256 on a per-interface basis. This feature should be disabled by setting the value to 0.
7	HKLM\System\CurrentControlSet\Services\Tcpip\Parameters\TcpMaxHalfOpen	100	This setting specifies the number of connections permitted in the SYN-RCVD state before SynAttackProtect measures are implemented.
8	HKLM\System\CurrentControlSet\Services\Tcpip\Parameters\TcpMaxHalfOpenRetried	80	This setting specifies the number of connections permitted in the SYN-RCVD state for which at least one retransmission of the SYN has been sent, before SynAttackProtect measures are implemented.
9	HKLM\System\CurrentControlSet\Services\Tcpip\Parameters\TCPMaxPortsExhausted	5	This setting specifies how many connection requests can be refused before SynAttackProtect measures are implemented.

---

[108] These settings will not appear in the Security Templates MMC snap-in.
[109] The recommendations apply to all the environments described in this publication.

6.9 Summary of Recommendations

- Establish account policies that reduce the likelihood of an attacker guessing or cracking passwords to gain unauthorized access to systems. The policies should balance security, functionality, and usability.

- Configure the audit policy to record certain types of activity to a log, so that system administrators can review the logs and detect unauthorized activity.

- Assign user rights following the principle of least privilege.

- Set additional security options to achieve greater security than the default options provide; examples include limiting the use of blank passwords, renaming the default Administrator and Guest accounts, and specifying which types of authentication may be used.

- Enable logging for the Application, Security, and System Logs.

- Remove all users from the Remote Desktop Users and Power Users groups that do not specifically need to be members.

- Disable all unnecessary services.

- Disable the Universal Plug and Play feature and the Remote Assistance feature unless they are needed.

- Use ACLs to restrict access to critical executables and registry entries.

- Set registry values that limit debugging and automatic execution of CD-ROM content, as well as configuring networking more securely.

- Review, customize, test, document, and deploy the NIST security templates or GPOs, as appropriate, to secure Windows XP systems.

7. Additional Windows XP Configuration Recommendations

The previous section of this guide discussed the configuration settings implemented by the NIST templates and GPOs. This section addresses additional security-related recommendations for Windows XP that are not included in the templates and GPOs. These recommendations should either be configured manually or applied with the aid of additional .inf or .adm files that are not provided by NIST. The recommendations address filesystem security issues, user accounts and groups, auditing, software restriction policies, network interfaces, Windows Firewall, and IPsec.

It is important to consider the concept of security for a Windows XP workstation as an ongoing task. The recommendations presented in this section and previous sections do not entail the complete set of possible security considerations and concerns for the entire life cycle of a Windows XP workstation. System administrators and end users should consider the effect that each decision made regarding a workstation might have on its security.

7.1 Filesystem Security

Filesystem security is a very important component of host security. This section describes the filesystems available in Windows XP—NTFS, File Allocation Table 16 (FAT16), and FAT32—and explains why NTFS should be used. The Folder Options section of Control Panel contains several settings that are related to filesystem security, such as determining which application should run a file based on its file extension; this section discusses those settings and recommends how they should be set. This information can be particularly helpful in preventing malware infections caused by running files with unusual file extensions. In addition, by default, Windows XP systems have registry settings that suppress the display of certain file extensions. This section explains how to find and delete the registry settings so that all filenames are displayed the same way, regardless of file extension. Another topic addressed in this section is supporting the confidentiality and integrity of data through Encrypting File System (EFS).

7.1.1 NTFS

In terms of security, the NTFS filesystem[110] is vastly superior to the other XP filesystem options—FAT16 and FAT32.[111] Neither FAT16 nor FAT32 provides features for establishing access control for files or encrypting files. Windows XP uses NTFS version 3.1; it is very similar to version 3.0, which is used by Windows 2000. The most notable new features in version 3.1 are disk quotas and file encryption.[112] NTFS can also provide highly granular access control for files, folders, and shares, as well as other resources on the system.

To verify that all disk partitions are formatted with NTFS, either use MBSA (described in Section 4.4) or perform the following steps:

1. Right-click **My Computer** and select **Manage**.

2. Select the **Disk Management** tool located under **Storage** to verify that the nonremovable partitions are using NTFS. For example, in Figure 7-1, the C: and D: drives are using NTFS, and the G: drive is using FAT32.

---

[110] More information on NTFS is available from the Microsoft article *How NTFS Works*, located at http://technet.microsoft.com/en-us/library/cc781134.aspx.

[111] For a comparison of filesystems, see Charlie Russel's article titled *NTFS vs. FAT: Which Is Right for You?*, available at http://www.microsoft.com/windowsxp/using/setup/expert/russel_october01_mspx.

[112] For more information on the new features in NTFS version 3.1, see MSKB article 310749, *New Capabilities and Features of the NTFS 3.1 File System*, available at http://support.microsoft.com/?id=310749.

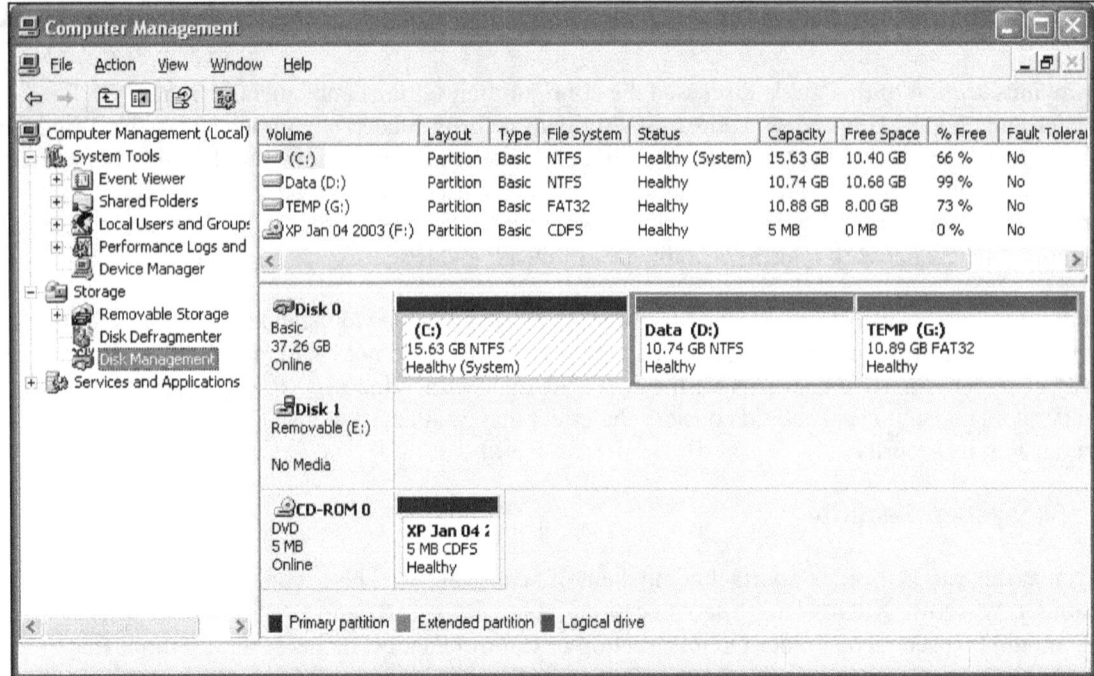

Figure 7-1. Disk Management

In enterprise, SSLF, and FDCC environments, NIST strongly recommends that existing systems based on FAT partitions should be rebuilt with NTFS, not converted from FAT to NTFS, because FAT-to-NTFS conversion does not set the NTFS permissions to the same default values as rebuilding a system with NTFS. In other environments, it is preferred to rebuild the system with NTFS, but it is also considered acceptable to perform a FAT to NTFS conversion. Perform the following steps to convert a FAT partition to NTFS:

1. Back up the system.

2. From the Start menu, choose **Run** and type **cmd.exe** to open a command prompt window.

3. Execute the **convert** command with the appropriate parameters. For example, the following command will convert the D drive to NTFS in a verbose mode: **convert D: /FS:NTFS /V**.

7.1.2 Folder Options

Modifying the Folder Options can greatly improve defenses against malware. The system can be configured to show all filenames fully, including their extensions. In addition, Folder Options contains the associations between file types and the default applications that run each file type. By modifying the associations for file extensions that are often used for malicious purposes, such files will be run by the Notepad application, which effectively neutralizes them. The Folder Options changes described below are highly recommended for every environment. The only caveat is that any file extensions that have a legitimate function in the organization should not be remapped to Notepad, or the functionality may be broken. Perform the following steps to modify the Folder Options:

1. Click the **Start** menu and choose **Control Panel**. Select **Folder Options**.

2. Verify that the **Show common tasks in folders**, **Open each folder in the same window**, and **Double-click to open an item (single-click to select)** radio buttons are selected.

3. Select the **View** tab. Adjust the settings so that they match the check boxes and radio buttons in Figure 7-2.

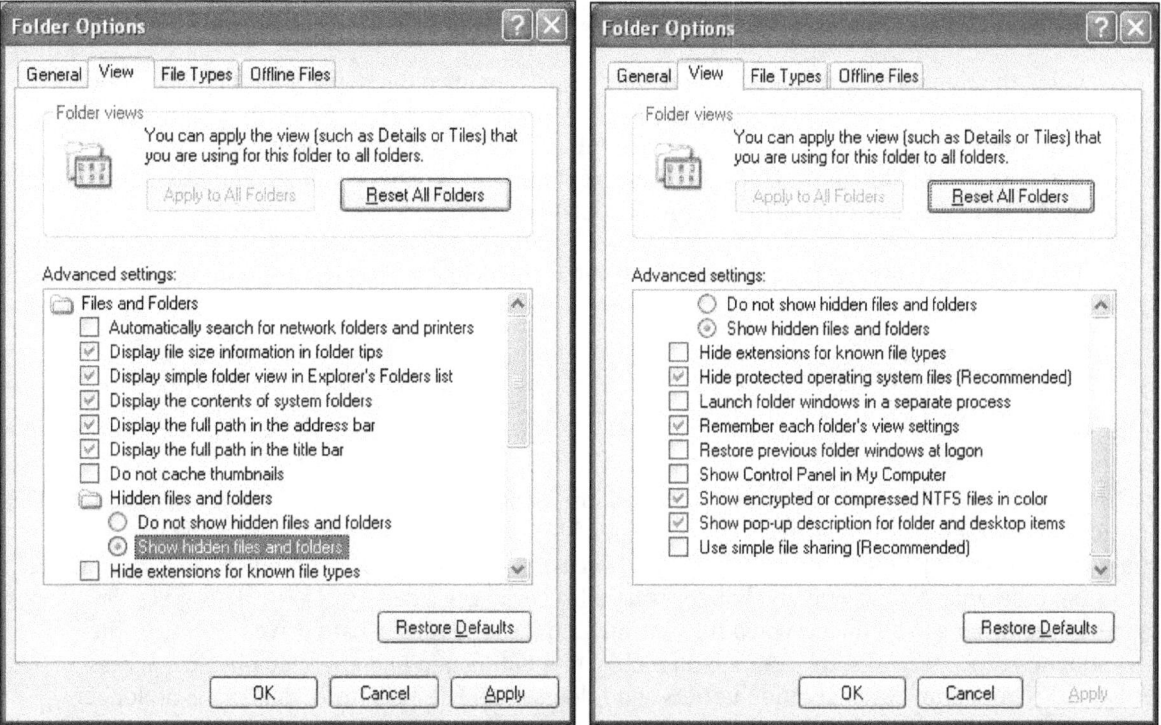

Figure 7-2. Folder Options Dialog Boxes

4. Select the **File Types** tab. Scroll down the registered file types window to select the **JS** extension and click the **Change** button.

5. Select the **Notepad** program and click **OK**.

6. Repeat the previous two steps to change the mapping for the following extensions: **JSE**, **OTF**, **REG**, **SCT**, **SHB**, **SHS**, **VBE**, **VBS**, **WSC**, **WSF**, and **WSH**.

7. Click the **Close** button and click **OK**.

7.1.3 Show Hidden File Types

Some file extensions will continue to remain hidden from the user, even when the **Hide file extension for known file types** setting is disabled. If the **NeverShowExt** registry value is set, Windows will hide the file extensions for basic Windows file types, regardless of other user configuration choices. For example, the **.lnk** extension associated with Windows shortcuts remains hidden even after a user has turned off the option to hide extensions. Attackers have taken advantage of this feature for several years by sending users malicious files that use one of the hidden file extensions.[113] The users do not see the file extension and are fooled into thinking the file is safe. Although it is strongly recommended from a security perspective to display all file extensions, and it will have no impact on system functionality, users may be confused by the change. For example, most icons on the Start menu will show a **.lnk** extension. In an enterprise, administrators may decide to compromise by showing all file extensions except **.lnk**.

To prevent all file extensions from being hidden, perform these steps:

1. Click the **Start** menu, select **Run**, and enter **regedit** to open the registry editor. Click **OK**.

2. Click the My Computer icon and press **Ctrl+F**. Clear the **Keys** and **Data** check boxes. Type in the value **NeverShowExt**. Click the **Find Next** button. When the value is found, right-click and select **Delete**. Click on **Yes** to confirm the deletion.

3. Press **F3** to find the next occurrence of the value and delete it. Repeat this until no occurrences are found.

4. Exit **regedit** and restart the computer.

7.1.4 EFS

The Encrypting File System (EFS) is designed to address numerous concerns regarding the integrity of data stored on Windows XP systems. EFS is designed to keep data private and unreadable to unauthorized users. Malicious users with physical access to a Windows XP computer can boot it into a file system other than NTFS, effectively bypassing all security provided by NTFS. This gives the malicious user access to all unencrypted files residing on the computer's hard drive. EFS uses file encryption to reduce the risks associated with mobile computing and unauthorized physical access. Because EFS only provides encryption to files and folders on NTFS partitions, the data is no longer protected when it is placed elsewhere (e.g., e-mail attachment, CD-ROM) or transmitted over the network. Other protection measures should be used, such as a virtual private network (VPN) or third-party file encryption software.

EFS, which is based on public-key encryption, integrates tightly with the public key infrastructure (PKI) features that have been incorporated into Windows XP. The actual logic that performs the encryption is a system service that cannot be shut down. This program feature is designed to prevent unauthorized access, but has an added benefit of rendering the encryption process completely transparent to the user. Each file that a user may encrypt is encrypted using a randomly generated file encryption key (FEK).

EFS can be used to encrypt individual files and folders on NTFS volumes.[114] The default configuration of EFS allows a user to encrypt and decrypt files immediately without any administrator interaction. When a folder is encrypted, all new files created there will be encrypted, as will any files moved there, so that users do not need to manually encrypt each new file. EFS can also encrypt shared files on a network resource and has the ability to decrypt the files even when not connected to that resource.

---

[113] One example of this is described in CERT®/CC Incident Note IN-2000-07, available at http://www.cert.org/incident_notes/IN-2000-07.html.

[114] One limitation of EFS to consider when choosing to encrypt an entire volume is that the volume upon which Windows XP is installed cannot be encrypted in its entirety because the EFS decryption routines are not available until late in the boot process. This would lead the OS to try to boot but fail because necessary parts of the OS were decrypted and could not be read to finish the boot process.

7.1.4.1 EFS Implementation Example

EFS can be implemented by three means: the **Properties** window of a folder, the **My Computer** window, and **Windows Explorer**. When implementing EFS, it is recommended that an encryption folder be created for sensitive files. This example process describes how to implement EFS for a sample folder from within the **My Computer** window.

1. From the **My Computer** window, create a new folder and name it **Sample Folder**.

2. Right-click on **Sample Folder** and click on **Properties**, then click the **Advanced** button. This should open the **Advanced Attributes** window.

3. Check the **Encrypt contents to secure data** box and click on **OK**. Click on **OK** again. The color of **Sample Folder** should have changed, indicating that all files added to this folder should automatically be encrypted.

4. Run Notepad and enter some text. Save the file as **Sample.txt** in **Sample Folder**.

5. Double click on **Sample Folder** to view its contents. The color of the **Sample.txt** file name should indicate that it is encrypted.

6. Right-click on **Sample.txt** and click on **Properties**, then click the **Advanced** button. This confirms that the file is encrypted.

7.1.4.2 EFS Data Recovery

The EFS process is transparent to the end user because EFS is integrated with NTFS. Other users with similar or lesser privileges could not open another user's EFS-encrypted file because they do not have the FEK. In some cases, access restrictions such as these require authorized users to implement data recovery procedures. For example, if the key-pair used to encrypt a file were corrupted, the file would be rendered inaccessible without a Data Recovery Agent (DRA).

Windows XP EFS provides integrated data recovery support. The Windows XP security infrastructure enforces the configuration of data recovery keys so well that EFS is inaccessible unless one or more recovery keys are created. This is typically done during the installation process. By default, the recovery agent is the **Administrator**. EFS will allow recovery agents to configure public keys that are used to enable file recovery. Only the file's randomly generated encryption key is available using the recovery key, not a user's private key. This action ensures that no other private information is revealed accidentally to the recovery agent. In a domain environment, the domain administrator can easily add an EFS recovery agent account to the role of a recovery agent via Group Policy. This feature can mitigate the risk of lost data as a result of the original user losing his decryption credentials. In a standalone environment, a recovery agent needs to be manually defined, or no one will be able to decrypt the information if encryption credentials are lost. EFS should not be used if a recovery agent has not been defined.

When considering implementing EFS in any environment, special consideration needs to be given to how keys and DRAs will be managed. If data needs to be retained for a long period of time while encrypted, long-term retention of appropriate keys to decrypt the data must be addressed. Depending on the nature of the information and the need to retain it, losing the ability to decrypt the files could seriously affect the mission of the organization. When considering the use of DRAs, it is essential that organizationally sensitive information not be accidentally disclosed to people who should not have access to the information.

The recovery keys contained in the **Encrypted Data Recovery Agents** folder can be backed up to removable media by logging into the system with the built-in **Administrator** account and performing the following actions:

1. Open the **Encrypted Data Recovery Agents** folder located within the **Group Policy** snap-in.

2. Right-click the Certificate that should be exported.

3. Choose **All Tasks**, then **Export**.

4. Save the file to removable media.

5. For maximum security, the EFS recovery certificate can be removed from the computer after a successful backup by selecting the **Delete Private Key if the Export is Successful** check box. This is highly recommended for mobile systems.

NIST recommends that EFS be deployed only when the confidentiality of the information in question is critical or when the system faces significant physical threats. For example, EFS may be a solution for securing data on mobile laptops that are at high risk of being stolen or lost and desktops that contain sensitive information. Any decisions on EFS deployment should take into account the key management issues discussed in this section. If key management is not handled effectively, the use of EFS could contribute to the loss of valuable information. EFS should definitely be considered for SOHO and SSLF environments; it may also be beneficial on some systems in enterprise and FDCC environments if key management can be handled well.

On systems that are using EFS, Syskey should also be used to establish a startup key that protects the private keys used for EFS.[115] By default on all Windows XP systems, Syskey is enabled and stores the machine-generated random key in pieces across the registry on the local system. An administrator can reconfigure Syskey to store the random key on a floppy disk instead of the local system, or to specify an administrator-chosen password as the key.[116] The system then cannot be booted without inserting the removable media or typing in the specified password, respectively.

7.1.5 Storage Device Sanitization and Disposal

Organizations should properly sanitize all storage devices, including fixed devices (e.g., hard drives) and removable devices and media (e.g., optical discs, magnetic disks, flash memory), before reusing them or disposing of them. If storage devices are not properly scrubbed of data, information could be accessed by unauthorized parties. Windows XP includes a command-line utility called **cipher** that is intended for use with EFS, but can also be used independent of EFS to scrub data from unused portions of disks.[117] By using the **/w** switch, an administrator can use cipher to do three passes. Although this may be convenient in some cases, it is generally recommended to acquire a third party tool that can do at least seven passes when overwriting data. Alternatives to overwriting data include degaussing and physical destruction of

---

[115] Microsoft recommends using Syskey with EFS in *Encrypting File System in Windows XP and Windows Server 2003*, located at http://technet.microsoft.com/en-us/library/bb457065.aspx.

[116] More information on changing the Syskey modes is available from MSKB article 143475 at http://support.microsoft.com/?id=143475.

[117] For more information on using the cipher utility to clear data, see the Microsoft article titled *Encrypting File System in Windows XP and Windows Server 2003*, which is available at http://technet.microsoft.com/en-us/library/bb457065.aspx.

storage devices.[118] Regardless of the method chosen, organizations should maintain a log that lists each cleaned device and documents how the data was removed.

7.2 User Accounts and Groups

This section discusses the importance of securing user accounts and groups. Windows XP installs several user accounts by default. To prevent misuse of these accounts, they should be disabled or replaced with equivalent accounts. In addition, administrative-level accounts should be used only for system administration tasks, which means that at least one user-level account should be created for daily operation of the system. Another important task is to create a password reset disk, which can be used to regain administrator-level access to the system if the administrator password is forgotten. The password reset disk should be stored in a physically secure location. (The use of password reset disks is not recommended for managed environments.) This section will discuss each of these topics.

7.2.1 Built-in Accounts

Default user accounts are often used in exploits against various computer systems, including Windows XP. By disabling default user accounts, it will be more difficult for attackers to gain access to a computer. This is not a foolproof solution, but it will discourage some attackers who would rather look for easy targets. The Guest account has historically been a common means by which to gain remote access to a computer, but it is disabled by default in Windows XP. Once an attacker has gained guest-level access, the attacker can try to elevate their privileges to further exploit the machine. Attackers also attempt to use the default Administrator account, so some organizations may choose to create a new account with Administrator-level privileges and then disable the original Administrator account. Normally, the user account created during installation has Administrator-level privileges, but this should still be verified.[119] NIST recommends that the built-in Administrator and Guest accounts be disabled and renamed on all Windows XP systems.[120] This can be done by modifying the NIST security templates or GPOs and pushing the settings down as a policy. To make the changes manually, perform the following steps:

1. Click the **Start** menu and select **Control Panel**. Double-click the **Administrative Tools** folder.

2. Double-click the **Computer Management** shortcut.

3. Expand the **Local Users and Groups** item and select the **Groups** folder.

4. A list of groups should be displayed in the right pane. Double-click the **Administrators** group.

5. Confirm that the group is composed of only two accounts: the built-in Administrator account, and the account that is being used to harden the system. If a user account is not present, create a user account and add it to the Administrators group. Do not disable the Administrator account until a user account has been added to the Administrators group. Upon completion, the Administrators group should contain only two accounts. Click **OK** to continue.

---

[118] More information on sanitizing, degaussing, and destroying storage devices is available from the Department of Defense's *National Industrial Security Program Operating Manual*, DoD 5220.22-M, located at http://www.dtic.mil/whs/directives/corres/html/522022m.htm, and from NIST SP 800-88, *Guidelines for Media Sanitization,* located at http://csrc.nist.gov/publications/PubsSPs.html.

[119] In managed environments, it is common for only security and system administrators to have administrator-level access to the system and for no one to have guest-level access. Users should be made aware of what they can and cannot do on their own systems (e.g., installing software) and instructed on how to request changes that require administrator-level access.

[120] Even if the built-in Administrator account is disabled, it can still be used to log on to the system if it is booted in Safe Mode.

6. Under **Local Users and Groups**, select the **Users** folder.

7. Right-click the **Administrator** account, select **Rename**, and enter the new name. Creating a relatively obscure name for the account makes it less likely to be targeted by an attacker.

8. Right-click the renamed administrative account, select **Set Password**, and assign a strong password composed of a mix of digits, special, and upper and lower case characters, as shown in Figure 7-3. Click **OK**.

Figure 7-3. Set Password Dialog Box

9. Double-click the renamed administrative account and delete the description field or enter a new description. Verify that the **User cannot change password**, **Password never expires**, and **Account is disabled** boxes are checked. Click **OK**.

10. Rename the Guest account and set a strong password for the default guest account, composed of digits, special, and upper and lower case characters.

11. Double-click the renamed guest account and verify that the **User cannot change password**, **Password never expires**, and **Account is disabled** boxes are checked. Delete the description field or enter a new description. Click **OK**.

12. Disable all other built-in accounts that are not needed. Table 7-1 lists all the default Windows XP accounts.[121] For each account, right-click on it, select **Properties**, check the **Account is disabled** box, and click **OK**.

---

[121] In Windows systems, each user account is associated with a unique security identifier (SID). Each SID is a sequence of letters and digits that can be used to identify an account even if the associated username has changed. For example, SID S-1-5-*domain*-500 is used by the Administrator account; even if Administrator is renamed, the SID remains the same. More information on Windows XP user accounts, including SIDs, is available from MSKB article 243330 at http://support.microsoft.com/?id=243330.

Table 7-1. Default User Accounts

User Account Name	Description	Default SID
Administrator	Built-in account for computer/domain administration	S-1-5-*domain*-500
Guest	Built-in account for guest access to the computer/domain	S-1-5-*domain*-501
HelpAssistant	Account required for providing remote assistance for the computer	N/A (variable)
SUPPORT_388945a0	Account for the Help and Support Service	N/A (variable)
User-created install account	Account initially created during the installation	N/A (variable)

NIST recommends that administrators periodically review user accounts and disable those that have been inactive for 90 days, as well as disabling temporary accounts after 30 days. Organizations should also follow procedures to disable accounts as soon as they are no longer needed (e.g., user leaves the organization, user's responsibilities change). Disabled accounts should be deleted after a specific period of time to release resources and prevent unneeded accounts from accidentally being re-enabled.

7.2.2 Built-in Groups

Windows XP has several groups that are known as special groups. Windows XP manages the memberships of these groups automatically. Two special groups are of particular interest from a security perspective: **Authenticated Users** and **Everyone**. **Authenticated Users** includes all accounts (except Guest and Anonymous accounts) that have been authenticated. **Everyone** includes all local and domain-based accounts that access the system. In earlier versions of Windows, Anonymous users were included in the Everyone group, which often gave unauthorized users access to systems. In Windows XP, Anonymous logins are no longer part of the Everyone group.

By default, Windows XP also contains several local groups. Local groups differ from special groups because administrators can manage the membership of each local group but cannot alter the membership of special groups. Table 7-2 describes each local group, explains the privileges associated with the group, and lists the accounts that belong to the group by default.

Table 7-2. Default Local Groups

Group Name	Description
Administrators	Administrators have complete and unrestricted access to the computer. The default members of this group are the built-in Administrator account and the account that was initially created on installation. Only those accounts that require administrator-level access should be members of this group.
Backup Operators	This group can override security restrictions for the sole purpose of backing up and restoring files, including files protected by EFS. There are no default members of this group. Users who back up their own data should not be placed in this group; the group is intended to be used by a backup administrator or automated backup process to preserve any and all data on the system, regardless of other security protections. Only trusted users and processes performing such backups should be placed in this group.
Guests	This group has the same access as the Users group, except that Guests cannot view the OS event logs. The Guest account is the only default member of this group.
HelpServicesGroup	Users in this group can troubleshoot problems by using certain utilities. These users can log on locally or remotely to the system. The Support account is the only group member by default. Only those accounts that are being used to provide support should belong to this group.

Group Name	Description
Network Configuration Operators	Members of this group have administrative privileges only for managing the configuration of networking features. There are no default members of this group.
Power Users	This group is granted some administrative privileges. The purpose of this group is to give Power Users rights that standard users do not have so that Power Users can run legacy applications. However, Power Users can often leverage their limited rights to gain full administrator rights. There are no default members of this group. NIST highly recommends that the Power Users group not be used and that the privileges granted to standard users be adjusted slightly if necessary to compensate for any legacy application needs.
Remote Desktop Users	This group has rights to log on to the computer remotely through Remote Desktop Services. There are no default members of this group. Only users who currently need to access the system through Remote Desktop should belong to this group.
Replicator	This group was used in Windows NT 4.0 to support file replication in a domain configuration. It is not used in Windows XP; there are no default members of this group, and it should remain empty.
Users	This group has restricted rights that should prevent members from changing the security posture of the system. Users have sufficient privileges to perform their authorized functions, but not enough privileges to gain access to other users' data or to damage other users' applications. The default members of this group are all Authenticated Users and INTERACTIVE users. In addition, when a new user account is created with the predefined Limited account type, it is placed in the Users group. All users who need standard access to the system should be placed in the Users group.

7.2.3 Daily Use Accounts

It is strongly recommended that an additional account belonging only to the Users group be created for each user and used to operate the box on a daily basis (e.g., checking e-mail, surfing the Web, operating office automation applications). Such an account is known as a daily use account or limited user account. Accounts belonging to the Administrators group should be used only to perform system management tasks, such as installing system updates and application software, managing user accounts, and modifying system and application settings. In addition, users should not share accounts; having a separate account for each user provides protection for data and supports accountability by tying actions to a specific user account, which is linked to a particular person. To create a new standard user account for daily use, perform the following steps:

1. Right-click in the right pane and select **New User**. Enter the user name, full name, and a description, and click the **Create** button. The user will be prompted to enter a password at the next logon.

2. Verify that the user belongs to only the **Users** group.

3. Assign a strong password to the administrative account, if that has not already been done.

    a. Click the **Start** menu, choose **Control Panel**, and click on **User Accounts**.

    b. Select the administrative account.

    c. Click **Change my password**.

    d. Type the current password, enter the new password and type it once more to confirm it. Click the **Change Password** button.

7.2.4 Local Session Protection

It is important to provide protection against unauthorized local access to Windows XP systems. One such control is to lock the current user's session through automatic or manual means. A screen saver can lock a session automatically after the system has been idle for a certain number of minutes, requiring the user's password to be entered before unlocking the system. NIST strongly recommends using a password-enabled screen saver on all Windows XP systems that need protected from unauthorized access. Settings for enabling and configuring the screen saver are included in the FDCC GPOs but not the NIST security templates. To manually configure a password-enabled screen saver, perform the following steps:

1. Right-click on the desktop and select **Properties**.

2. Click on the **Screen Saver** tab.

3. Set the **Screen saver** to something other than **(None)**.

4. Set the **Wait** time to a maximum of 15 minutes.

5. Check the box marked **On resume, password protect** to require the user's password to unlock the system.

6. Click **OK**.

There are several ways in which users can manually lock their sessions. The simplest method is to hold down the **Windows logo** key on the keyboard and then press the **L** key. This locks the system and displays the **Unlock Computer** dialog box, which prompts the user to enter a username and password to unlock the system. Other methods of locking sessions are dependent on settings for the Welcome screen and Fast User Switching features, which are related to logging in to Windows XP systems. When the Welcome screen is enabled, usernames are displayed on the screen, and a person clicks on the appropriate username and types in a password to log in. When the Welcome screen is disabled, users have to type in their usernames instead of clicking on them. As described in Section 3.1.2, the Fast User Switching (FUS) feature is only available if the Welcome screen is enabled and the system is not part of a domain. Under those circumstances, FUS can be enabled or disabled. FUS allows two users to be logged on simultaneously by using the Switch User feature; however, the current user does not have access to the other user's session.

To enable or disable the Welcome screen and FUS features, perform the following steps:

1. From the **Start** menu, choose **Control Panel**.

2. Click on **User Accounts**, then click on **Change the way users log on or off**.

3. Check or uncheck the options called **Use the Welcome screen** and **Use Fast User Switching** as appropriate, then click on **Apply Options**.

If the Welcome screen is disabled, the user can lock the system by hitting CTRL+ALT+DEL to open the **Windows Security** dialog box, then clicking on the **Lock Computer** box. This locks the session and displays the **Unlock Computer** dialog box.

7.2.5 Password Reset Disk

For a system in a non-managed environment, a password reset disk could be created for the administrative account and stored in a physically secure area. The disk can be used if the password for the administrative account is forgotten or otherwise lost. If a current password reset disk is unavailable and no one can gain administrative access to the system, the system will likely need to be rebuilt at some point (unless a third-party tool is used to reset the account password).[122] For example, it may no longer be possible to keep the system patched and updated; also, if a user account becomes locked because of too many failed login attempts, it may not be possible to unlock it. Having a password reset disk is most important for systems that have only one enabled administrator account or contain important data, such as typical SOHO systems, as well as systems using EFS. In managed environments, particularly those in which data is not supposed to be stored on desktop systems, password reset disks are often not used. The administrative overhead of creating and storing tens of thousands of password reset disks is unreasonable, and often a domain administrator account also has access to the system. For environments in which a password reset disk is needed, perform the following steps to create it:

1. From the **Start** menu, choose **Control Panel**.

2. Click on **User Accounts**, then select the administrative account.

3. In the Related Tasks box, click on the **Prevent a forgotten password** link.

4. The Forgotten Password Wizard should start. Click on **Next**.

5. Select the **3 1/2 Floppy (A:)** drive as the destination where the password key will be stored and click **Next**.

6. Enter the current administrator password and click **Next**.

7. The wizard creates the disk. When the creation is completed, click **Next**.

8. When the wizard has completed, click **Finish**.

9. Store the password disk in a physically secure area.

Should the administrative account password be forgotten, perform the following steps to use the password reset disk:

1. At the logon screen, select the administrative account and press the Enter key or click the **right arrow** button located to the right of the password field.

2. Click the **Use your password reset disk** link.

3. Click **Next**.

4. Select the **3 1/2 Floppy (A:)** drive and click **Next**.

5. Enter the new password, retype it again to confirm, and click **Next**.

6. Click **Finish**.

---

[122] Using a third-party tool to reset the password for an account will render EFS data for that account inaccessible.

7. At the logon screen, select the administrator account and enter the newly created password to authenticate.

8. The current Password Reset Disk is no longer valid. Recreate the Password Reset Disk so that it contains the new password.

7.3 Auditing

Section 6.2.1 describes some of Windows XP's system auditing capabilities. Windows XP can also audit other things, such as actions performed on individual files in an NTFS filesystem. For example, auditing could be configured to log all successful and failed changes to operating system and application program files, or to log all accesses to critical data files. This section discusses file auditing and also explains how to access the Event Viewer, a tool for reviewing audit logs. Another topic addressed in this section is the importance of time synchronization to auditing.

7.3.1 Individual File Auditing

Windows XP provides a method to monitor access to any file stored on an NTFS-formatted partition. This auditing method is typically used to monitor access to sensitive files. To configure individual file auditing, perform the following steps:

1. Right-click on the file, and then select **Properties**.

2. Select the **Security** tab and click on **Advanced**.

3. Select the **Auditing** tab and click on **Add** to specify a user or group.

4. As shown in Figure 7-4, select the file permission access attributes that should be audited by clicking in the appropriate **Successful** and **Failed** check boxes.

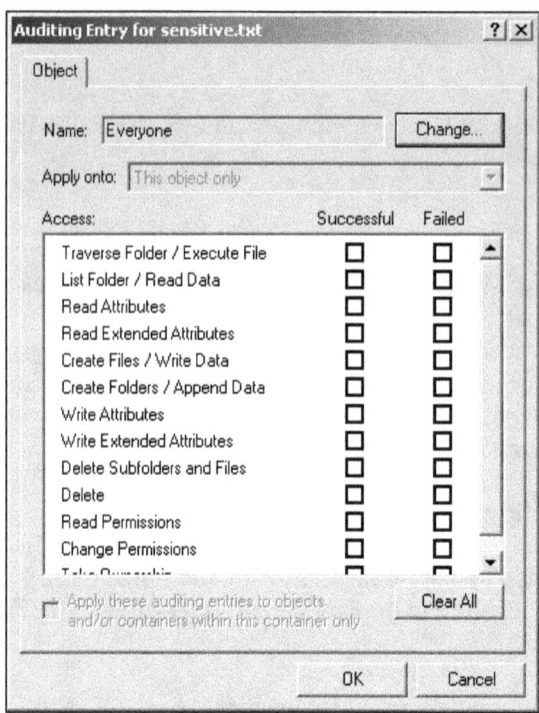

Figure 7-4. File Auditing

5. The output of the system auditing can be viewed using the Event Viewer, as described in Section 7.3.2.

7.3.2 Reviewing Audit Logs

Windows XP includes a built-in MMC snap-in tool called **Event Viewer** for reviewing application, security, and system logs. These logs contain audit records, among other types of information. The logs on each system should be reviewed on a regular basis to identify anomalous activity.[123] In enterprise and FDCC environments, this process should be automated through the use of special software on each system, such as a host-based intrusion detection system that monitors the logs, or through the use of centralized log servers that receive copies of the log entries from each system and analyze them for signs of suspicious activity.

To manually review audit logs using the Event Viewer, perform the following steps:

1. From the **Start** menu, choose **Control Panel**.

2. Select **Administrative Tools**, and then choose **Computer Management**.

3. Expand the **System Tools** listing, and then expand the **Event Viewer**. This displays the three types of logs: **Application**, **Security**, and **System**. Review the audit records, which are stored in the **Security** log.

---

[123] In SSLF environments, audit logs should be reviewed at least weekly, preferably daily.

7.3.3 Time Synchronization

It is important to configure Windows XP systems to synchronize their clocks on a regular basis with accurate time sources. If audit logs contain evidence of an attack and the system's clock is inaccurate, it makes the analysis of the attack more difficult and may also weaken the evidentiary value of the logs. Time synchronization is also convenient because users do not need to manually adjust the clock to compensate for inaccuracies in the system's timekeeping. Windows XP uses the Network Time Protocol (NTP) for time synchronization. By default, systems that participate in an Active Directory (AD) synchronize automatically with the domain controller (DC). To configure a Windows XP system that is not an AD member to perform time synchronization, perform the following steps:

1. From the **Start** menu, choose **Control Panel**.

2. Select **Date and Time**. Click on the **Internet Time** tab.

3. Check the **Automatically synchronize with an Internet time server** check box.

4. Enter the name or IP address of a time server (e.g., time-a.nist.gov). Most enterprise environments have one or more internal time servers; if such a server is available, it should be specified instead of an external time server.

5. Click on **Update Now** to confirm that time synchronization is working properly.

6. Click on **OK**.

7.4 Software Restriction Policy

Software restriction policies provide administrators with a policy-driven mechanism that identifies software running on their systems and controls the ability of that software to execute. Using a software restriction policy, an administrator can prevent unwanted applications from running, including viruses and Trojan horses, as well as software that is known to cause conflicts when installed. A software restriction policy is either set to Unrestricted or Disallowed. The Unrestricted setting allows all programs to run except those that are specified as forbidden. This is best suited to organizations in which users require great flexibility in which programs they can execute. By defining known problematic software, unapproved applications, and known Trojan horses, this setting can protect a host from known threats. The Disallowed setting means that no programs can run except those on the list of programs that are allowed to run. This is much more labor intensive because all needed applications must be identified, but it provides excellent protection against unapproved programs executing. The Disallowed setting is generally appropriate only for the highest security need situations, while the Unrestricted setting is better suited for blocking certain undesirable applications. Software restriction policies are most likely to be used in SSLF environments.

The Software Restriction Policy has five components:

- **Security Levels.** This is used to set the default rule as **Disallowed** or **Unrestricted**.

- **Additional Rules.** This lists all exceptions to the default rule. The rules can only reference files listed as Designated File Types. In addition, when more than one rule has been defined that would match a given program, the first matching rule will be selected.

- **Enforcement.** This item provides options regarding the policies. One option will apply the policy not only to executables, but also to dynamic link library (DLL) files. This option is set by selecting **Apply software restriction policies to the following**, then **All software files**. Another option allows local administrators to run software that other users cannot. This option is set by selecting **Apply software restriction policies to the following users**, then **All users except local administrators**.

- **Designated File Types.** This provides a way to tell the software restriction policies, which file extensions indicate an executable. By default, several common executable file extensions are already set. File extensions can be added and deleted from the list as needed.

- **Trusted Publishers.** This lists the software publishers that are trusted, such as local administrators. The system can verify the authenticity of the publisher's digital certificate before adding the publisher to the Trusted Publishers list.

To create and configure a software restriction policy, perform the following steps:

1. Log in as a local administrator or domain administrator, or as a user who has been delegated the authority to create software restriction policies.

2. Click **Start,** then select **Run.** In the **Open** field, type **mmc** and click **OK.**

3. The **Console** window will now appear. Click on **File**, then **Add/Remove Snap-in**, then **Add.** Select **Group Policy** and click on **Add**.

4. Click **Finish.**

5. In the Console window, expand **Local Computer Policy**, then **Computer Configuration**, then **Windows Settings**, then **Security Settings.**

6. If the **Security Settings** folder does not contain **Software Restriction Policies**, a new policy must be created. To do so, click **Action,** then select **Create New Policies**. Return to the **Security Settings** folder.

7. From the **Security Settings** folder, click on **Software Restriction Policies** and then the **Security Levels** folder. If the **Security Levels** folder does not exist, a new policy must be created. To do so, click **Action,** then select **Create New Policies**, and enter the **Security Levels** folder.

8. There are two options: Disallowed (software will not run, regardless of the access rights of the user), and Unrestricted (software access rights are determined by the access rights of the user.) Double-click on **Disallowed**. Click **Set as Default**, and then click **OK** to continue.

9. To open the **Local Security Policy,** click on **Start,** then click **Control Panel.** Click **Administrative Tools**, and then click **Local Security Policy**. This should open the Local Security Settings window.

10. Expand **Software Restrictions Policies** and click on the **Additional Rules** folder. The right pane should show the four default rules.

11. Right-click on the background of the right pane and add rules appropriate to the installation from the following choices:

- **Certificate Rule.** A Certificate Rule uses a certificate to verify the authenticity of the program to be run. By default, certificate-based **Software Policy** rules are disabled. To enable **Certificate Rules,** edit the registry as follows:

    - Click **Start**, click **Run**, type **regedit**, and then click **OK**.

    - Edit the key **HKEY_LOCAL_MACHINE\SOFTWARE\Policies\Microsoft\Windows\Safer\Code Identifiers**.

    - Select the value **AuthenticodeEnabled** and change the value data from **0** to **1**.

    - Click **OK,** then click **File** and **Exit** to close **regedit**.

- **Hash Rule.** The Hash Rule only allows a program to execute if the hash for that file matches the known good hash that the OS is expecting. This protects against a program being replaced by a modified version containing malware. Hashes are not dependent on the filename or location; therefore, if a file is renamed or moved, execution will still be permitted or denied based on the hash. If the size of the file changes, the hash will become invalid, and execution will be denied. It may be resource-intensive to identify all programs that may be needed on each system and to maintain and distribute current hashes for all programs.

- **Internet Zone Rule.** This rule applies to Windows Installer packages only. It provides a way to restrict what software can be run from remote sites.

- **Path Rule.** The Path Rule permits the user to designate files that are allowed to run based on path restrictions. The path can be an entire directory or a specific file. When defining a Path Rule, special consideration should be taken when the security level is set to **Disallowed** and the path specifies the Windows folder because this might prevent the execution of programs essential to Windows XP. One crucial limitation of the Path Rule is that if an entire directory has been defined, all programs located in that directory will be allowed to execute. This means that malicious or unauthorized programs placed in the authorized path will execute.

7.5 Securing Network Interfaces

By default, Windows XP includes a number of network protocols and components that are not usually required in all environments. For example, the File and Printer Sharing for Microsoft Networks service and the Client for Microsoft Networks are included in most Windows XP installations. These features allow the user to share resources on a network with other Windows systems, but they may increase the system's exposure level. The user should operate the system with only the necessary network protocols and disable the Microsoft networking client/server components if they are not being used.

7.5.1 Unneeded Networking Components

As previously discussed in Section 4.1.2.1, network clients, services, and protocols that are not needed should be disabled. This reduces the likelihood that the system will be compromised or misused. Use caution when disabling any network components, because this can cause required functionality to break, sometimes in unexpected ways. The following components are candidates for being disabled:

- The **QoS Packet Scheduler** is designed to prioritize network traffic by application or service over slow network connections. Most applications are not QoS-aware, and some are incompatible with

QoS, so the QoS Packet Scheduler is not beneficial in most situations. In general, the QoS Packet Scheduler should be disabled unless testing in a specific environment demonstrates that it is beneficial at alleviating network bandwidth issues.

- Uninstalling the **File and Printer Sharing for Microsoft Networks** service will prevent other systems from connecting to the local file and printer shares; it will not prevent users of the local system from connecting to remote file and printer shares. Therefore, leave this service installed only if the local system shares its resources (e.g., files, printers) and users on other systems need to connect to these resources through the network, or necessary applications (e.g., MBSA, remote administration) require the service.

- Uninstalling the **Client for Microsoft Networks** will prevent the local system from establishing network connections to other systems' Microsoft file and printer shares. Most systems will require the client to be enabled, so it should generally be disabled only if the system has particularly high security needs.

To disable any of these components, perform the following steps:

1. Click the **Start** menu, choose **Control Panel**, select **Network Connections**, and double-click on **Local Area Connection**.

2. Click the **Properties** button.

3. Select the component and click the **Uninstall** button.

4. Click **Yes** to proceed.

7.5.2 Use of Port 445

If the system needs to connect to other Windows systems' file shares, it can use either the traditional port 139 or the new port 445. By default, it will try to connect on port 139 before trying port 445, so disabling port 445 should result in exposing only the conventional port 139. Before implementing this system modification, refer to local policies to confirm that it is acceptable and appropriate for the environment. Also, by default, Windows Firewall blocks all incoming network traffic destined for port 445. To disable the use of port 445, perform the following steps:

1. Click the **Start** menu and select **Run**. Open **regedit** and click **OK**.

2. Locate the following entry:
   HKEY_LOCAL_MACHINE\SYSTEM\CurrentControlSet\Services\NetBT\Parameters.

3. Right-click in the right pane, select **New**, and click **DWORD value**. Name the value **SmbDeviceEnabled** and assign it a value of **0**.

4. Exit **regedit**.

7.5.3 TCP/IP Configuration

The default TCP/IP configuration contains a few settings that should be altered to improve security. However, each setting could have a negative effect on the functionality that the system provides, so it is very important to understand the impact of changing each setting. The following steps for altering the settings include an explanation of the significance of each setting:

1. Click the **Start** menu, choose **Control Panel**, select **Network Connections**, and double-click on **Local Area Connection**.

2. Click the **Properties** button.

3. Select **Internet Protocol (TCP/IP)** and click the **Properties** button.

4. Click the **Advanced** button.

5. Select the **DNS** tab and uncheck the **Register this connection's addresses in DNS** box. If the system is registered in DNS, this could unnecessarily provide information about the system to an unauthorized party who can access DNS information. However, disabling this setting on an AD member will prevent the system from working properly.

6. Select the **WINS** tab. Uncheck the **Enable LMHOSTS lookup** box unless it is needed for compatibility with legacy systems.

7. Select the radio button marked **Disable NetBIOS over TCP/IP** unless this functionality is required by the system. Generally, NetBIOS over TCP/IP is only needed if the system needs to communicate with legacy systems running Windows NT, Windows 95, or Windows 98. If NetBIOS over TCP/IP is enabled, the system's resources may be exposed to network-based attacks.

8. Click **OK**, then **OK**, then **Close**.

7.6 Windows Firewall

Windows Firewall is the built-in Windows XP stateful firewall.[124] It can be configured to restrict all inbound connections, but cannot filter or block any outbound connections. Windows Firewall tracks traffic that originates from the local host by maintaining a table of all the communications. An inbound packet is permitted if a matching entry in the table shows that the network connection has been initiated from the local host. The primary benefit of Windows Firewall is in limiting network connections to a computer, thus reducing the exposure of the computer to network-based attacks, such as worms.

Windows Firewall is enabled by default for each network interface. This provides immediate protection from network-based attacks for all network connections, including LAN (wired and wireless), dial-up, and VPN. Unfortunately, by default it may also inadvertently break needed functionality. For example, Windows Firewall blocks all incoming traffic directed at TCP port 445, which may prevent administrators from using various MMC snap-ins to administer the system remotely.[125] Also, if it is not configured correctly, Windows Firewall can also prevent the use of Microsoft file and print services, as well as other services and applications. If Windows Firewall and a third party host-based firewall are both enabled, Windows Firewall might block traffic that the other firewall has been configured to allow, impacting system functionality and usability. Windows Firewall can also increase the difficulty of troubleshooting

---

[124] Windows Firewall was added to Windows XP in Service Pack 2. Before SP2, the built-in firewall was called the Internet Connection Firewall (ICF). For more information on ICF, read MSKB article 320855, *Description of the Windows XP Internet Connection Firewall*, available at http://support.microsoft.com/?id=320855.

[125] Administrators can create exception rules for Windows Firewall in Group Policy, so that the firewall will allow administrators to connect to the Windows XP system on specific ports from specific management hosts.

problems with connecting to network services. Another potential problem is that some people might get a false sense of security from the presence of Windows Firewall and not maintain the security of the system properly (e.g., not applying security patches).

When enabled and configured correctly, Windows Firewall offers several benefits, including the following:

- Allowing certain types of traffic from the local subnet only. By default, when Microsoft networking services are enabled, Windows Firewall configures itself so that the appropriate ports (UDP 137, UDP 138, TCP 139, and TCP 445) will only accept packets that have a source address on the local subnet. If UPnP is enabled, Windows Firewall establishes similar restrictions for the UPnP ports (UDP 1900 and TCP 2869). Because Microsoft networking services and UPnP should normally be used only between computers on a local network, this firewall policy should not interfere with typical functionality. It also restricts the ability of remote attackers and malware from breaching these services.

- Permitting only typical boot-time traffic (e.g., DHCP) during boot. This is possible because Windows Firewall is loaded before the TCP/IP stack. Limiting activity during boot protects the system against network-based attacks (particularly worms that constantly send malicious packets) that occur during the seconds or minutes it takes for the system to boot.

- Configuring it partially during unattended setup and fully through Group Policy. This is most beneficial for securing workstations in enterprise environments, particularly managed environments. Windows Firewall can also be configured through a command-line interface.

- Providing a single interface for firewalling IPv4 and IPv6 traffic.

- Allowing the creation of multiple firewall profiles. For example, a laptop could use a less restrictive profile when on the enterprise LAN, and a more restrictive profile when directly connected to the Internet.

- Specifying which programs can use particular ports.

When a Windows XP Professional computer is a member of a domain, the domain administrator can enable Group Policy that prevents the use of Windows Firewall while the computer is connected to the corporate network. This enables the laptop to use enterprise network resources with no added complexity for the user or the network administrator. When the laptop is being used at home or a public Internet connection hot spot, Windows Firewall is available because Group Policy does not apply.

Despite the possible drawbacks of Windows Firewall, the security benefits (e.g., reducing exposure to new worms, giving system administrators more time to apply certain patches) outweigh them, so NIST recommends implementing Windows Firewall. However, Windows Firewall should not be implemented if a third-party firewall is already being used to protect the system. To enable and configure Windows Firewall, perform the following steps:

1. Click the **Start** menu and choose **Control Panel**. Double-click **Windows Firewall**.

2. Ensure that the firewall is set to **On**.

3. Click the **Exceptions** tab. Verify that only the needed services are checked (enabled).

4. Click the **Advanced** tab. Verify that the check boxes are selected for each network interface.

5. Click the **Settings** button for ICMP. Verify that none of the check boxes are selected, then click on **OK**.

6. Click the **Settings** button for Security Logging. Check the **Log dropped packets** and **Log successful connections** boxes. Enter 32767 KB in the **Size limit** field. Click **OK**.

7. By default, the log file **pfirewall.log** is located in the **C:\Windows** directory. The log file is text-based and contains several pieces of data for each log entry, including the date and time the packet was received, the status (e.g., connection opened, closed, dropped), the IP, the source and destination IP addresses and ports, the packet size, various TCP header values, and the ICMP type and code. The log file should be reviewed periodically to look for suspicious network activity.

The FDCC GPOs contain security settings for Windows Firewall. Additional guidance on configuring Windows Firewall is available from the Microsoft Web site.[126]

In SSLF environments or other situations where tracking network activity is particularly important, the Microsoft-provided Port Reporter service may be useful.[127] It can log TCP and UDP port usage, the processes associated with each port, and other related information. The log entries created by Port Reporter may be very helpful when investigating an incident or troubleshooting network application-related problems.

7.7 IPsec

IPsec is designed to encrypt data as it travels between two computers or a computer and a gateway, protecting the data from modification and interpretation.[128] IPsec filtering can also be used to control network traffic flows by restricting and allowing unencrypted traffic for specific ports and protocols. For example, IPsec filtering (as well as network device filters, such as firewall rulesets or router access control lists) could permit Microsoft networking protocols (e.g., CIFS) to be used only with certain trusted hosts, or to prevent the use of applications such as instant messaging and peer-to-peer file sharing that use known port numbers.[129] Using IP filtering, IPsec examines all IP packets for addresses, ports, and transport protocols. Rules contained in local or group policies tell IPsec to ignore or secure specific packets, depending on addressing and protocol information.

By default, certain traffic is not filtered or protected by Windows XP IPsec. These kinds of traffic are known as the *default exemptions* and, minus broadcast and multicast, they only apply to IPsec transport mode filters:

- **Resource Reservation Protocol (RSVP).** Used for QoS of IP traffic. Required for QoS to work with Windows XP.

---

[126] http://technet.microsoft.com/en-us/library/cc737845.aspx
[127] More information on installing, configuring, and using the Port Reporter service is available from MSKB article 837243, *Availability and description of the Port Reporter tool*, at http://support.microsoft.com/?id=837243. This article also provides a link to where Port Reporter is available for download.
[128] For more information on IPsec, consult NIST SP 800-77, *Guide to IPsec VPNs*, available at http://csrc.nist.gov/publications/PubsSPs.html.
[129] Some applications use dynamic port numbers, which IPsec filtering cannot address effectively. Also, some applications can use well-known port numbers, such as a peer-to-peer file sharing application that functions on port 80, which is normally associated with Web traffic. Blocking the use of such a port could inadvertently break necessary functionality. A proxying firewall may be effective at identifying and stopping the use of undesired applications, regardless of the ports they use.

- **Internet Key Exchange (IKE)**. IKE source and destination User Datagram Protocol (UDP) port 500 traffic used in many VPN configurations.

- **Kerberos**. Main authentication protocol used in native Windows XP domain environments. Kerberos traffic uses TCP and UDP source and destination port 88.

- **Broadcast**. Network traffic going from one sender to many receivers. Used for various networking functions.

- **Multicast**. Traffic sent from one sender to multiple receivers in the address range of 224.0.0.0 to 239.255.255.255.

A DWORD registry value can be set to remove most of these exemptions and allow filtering on the above traffic. The **HKLM\SYSTEM\CurrentControlSet\Services\IPSec\NoDefaultExempt** key can be set to 0 (default exemptions are still active) or 1 (disable the exemption for RSVP and Kerberos). Broadcast and multicast traffic cannot be restricted.

The steps to add or edit IPsec filters are listed below.

1. In **IP Security Policies** from the **Local Security Policy** tool, double-click the policy that should be modified.

2. To add an **IPsec filter list**, click Add on the **IP filter list** tab. To reconfigure an existing **IP filter list**, double-click the **IP filter list**.

3. In **IP Filter List**, do one of the following:

    - To use the IP Filter Wizard to create a filter, confirm that the **Use Add Wizard** check box is selected, and then click **Add**.

    - To create a filter manually, clear the **Use Add Wizard** check box, then click **Add**.

    - To reconfigure an existing filter, double-click the filter.

4. On the **Addressing** tab, select the **Source Address** as shown in Table 7-3:

Table 7-3. Enable TCP/IP Port Filtering

Select	To Secure Packets From
My IP Address	All IP addresses on the computer for which the filter is being configured.
Any IP Address	Any computer.
A specific DNS Name	The Domain Name System (DNS) name specified in *Host name*. The DNS name is resolved to its IP addresses, and then filters are automatically created for the resolved IP addresses. This option is available only when creating new filters.
A Specific IP Address	The IP address specified in *IP Address*.
A Specific IP Subnet	The IP address specified in *IP Address* and subnet mask specified in *Subnet Mask*.

5. Click **Destination Address** and repeat the previous step for the destination address.

6. Under **Mirrored**, select the appropriate setting from the following list:

    – To automatically create two filters based on the filter settings (one for traffic to the destination and one for traffic from the destination), select the **Mirrored** check box.

    – To create a single filter based on the filter settings, clear the **Mirrored** check box.

    – To create a filter for an IPsec tunnel, clear the **Mirrored** check box. Create two filter lists: one that describes the traffic to be sent through the tunnel (outbound traffic) and another that describes the traffic to be received through the tunnel (inbound traffic). Then create two rules that use the inbound and outbound filter lists in the policy.

7. On the **Description** tab, in **Description**, type a description for this filter; for example, specify to which computers and traffic types it applies.

8. If additional IP filtering by a specific protocol or port number is required, configure advanced filter settings on the **Protocol** tab.

7.8 Wi-Fi Network Configuration

Windows XP provides built-in support for wireless networking (also known as wireless fidelity, or Wi-Fi).[130] By default, Windows XP systems use Wi-Fi in *infrastructure mode*, which means that they are clients connecting to a wireless access point (AP). (The alternative is *ad hoc mode*, which means that wireless clients connect to each other without an AP. Ad hoc mode is rarely used.) The most commonly used Wi-Fi protocol, IEEE 802.11b, relies on the Wired Equivalent Privacy (WEP) protocol, which has several known security issues. To provide a more secure Wi-Fi solution, an industry group called the Wi-Fi Alliance has created a product certification called Wi-Fi Protected Access (WPA).[131] WPA requires stronger security than WEP provides, including more robust authentication and key management, mandatory encryption (including optional AES support), and data integrity checking. NIST recommends that Windows XP Wi-Fi users use a stronger security solution than WEP whenever possible.[132] For WPA, this involves installing a new network adapter driver on each Windows XP system, updating APs to support WPA, and configuring Wi-Fi clients and APs to take advantage of WPA's features.[133]

---

[130] For more information on general Wi-Fi security, see NIST SP 800-48 Revision 1, *Guide to Securing Legacy IEEE Wireless Networks* and NIST SP 800-97, *Establishing Wireless Robust Security Networks: A Guide to IEEE 802.11i* (http://csrc.nist.gov/publications/PubsSPs.html). Windows-specific Wi-Fi references include *Securing Wireless LANs with Certificate Services* (http://www.microsoft.com/technet/security/prodtech/windowsserver2003/pkiwire/swlan.mspx?mfr=true) and *Securing Wireless LANs with PEAP and Passwords* (http://www.microsoft.com/downloads/details.aspx?FamilyID=60c5d0a1-9820-480e-aa38-63485eca8b9b&displaylang=en).

[131] More information on WPA is available from http://www.microsoft.com/windowsxp/using/networking/security/wireless.mspx.

[132] FIPS 140-2, *Security Requirements for Cryptographic Modules*, is mandatory and binding for federal agencies that have determined that certain information be protected via cryptographic means. For more information about FIPS-validated products, visit http://csrc.nist.gov/groups/STM/index.html. WPA does not require FIPS-approved encryption algorithms, but its successor, WPA2, does. WPA2 is based on IEEE 802.11i. Organizations should carefully consider the use of products with WPA2 certification and products that support IEEE 802.11i instead of the non-FIPS-approved algorithms provided by SP2. For more information on SP3's support of WPA and WPA2, see Appendix B.

[133] The Microsoft TechNet article titled *Wireless Deployment Technology and Component Overview* (http://technet.microsoft.com/en-us/library/bb457015.aspx) provides detailed guidance on establishing and securing wireless connections. The Microsoft TechNet article titled *Configuring Windows XP IEEE 802.11 Wireless Networks for the Home and Small Business* provides a good overview of the topic; it is available at http://www.microsoft.com/technet/network/wifi/wifisoho.mspx.

7.9 Memory Files

On Windows XP systems, the contents of memory may be stored to various types of files, including memory dump files, paging files, and hibernation files. Each of these files may inadvertently record sensitive information (e.g., passwords, decrypted data) that could subsequently be retrieved by an attacker. As described below, restricting the use or retention of these files can help to prevent unauthorized access to systems and data:

- **Memory Dump File.** A *memory dump file* is created during an error condition to store the contents of memory. Unless specifically needed for troubleshooting purposes, dump files should not be created.[134] This action can be accomplished by doing the following:

    1. Open the **Control Panel** and select **System**. Select the **Advanced** tab.

    2. In the **Startup and Recovery** section of the **Advanced** tab, click the **Settings** button.

    3. In **Write Debugging Information**, select **(none)** from the drop down list. Click **OK**.

- **Paging File.** A *paging file* is a file that holds some of the contents of Windows XP's memory. This could include sensitive information. When the system is shut down and restarted, Windows XP does not reuse the old contents of the paging file. An attacker that gains physical access to the machine could potentially access sensitive information in the paging file, so organizations should configure Windows XP to clear it every time the system is shut down.[135] However, this slows system reboots, particularly on systems with large amounts of RAM. Section 6.2.3 has instructions for setting this security option manually.

- **Hibernation File.** A *hibernation file* is created to preserve the current state of a system (typically a laptop) by recording memory and open files before shutting off the system. When the system is next turned on, the state of the system is restored. Organizations may want to consider disabling the use of hibernation files for SSLF systems. To do so, perform the following steps:

    1. Open the **Control Panel**.

    2. Click on **Power Options** and then click on the **Hibernate** tab.

    3. Uncheck the **Enable hibernate** option, and click **Apply**.

7.10 Summary of Recommendations

- In enterprise, SSLF, and FDCC environments, rebuild existing systems based on FAT partitions with NTFS, instead of converting FAT to NTFS.

- Modify the **Folder Options** to improve defenses against malware by showing all filenames fully and modifying the associations for file extensions often used for malicious purposes.

---

[134] For more information, see MSKB article 307973, *How to configure system failure and recovery options in Windows*, available at http://support.microsoft.com/?id=307973, and article 254649, *Overview of memory dump file options for Windows Server 2003, Windows XP, and Windows 2000*, available at http://support.microsoft.com/?id=254649.

[135] For more information, see MSKB article 314834, *How to Clear the Windows Paging File at Shutdown*, available at http://support.microsoft.com/?id=314834.

- Deploy EFS when the confidentiality of the information in question is critical or when the system faces significant physical threats. Any EFS deployment should take into account key management issues; if key management is not handled effectively, the use of EFS could contribute to the loss of valuable information. On systems that are using EFS, use Syskey to establish a startup key that protects the private keys used for EFS.

- Sanitize all storage devices, including fixed devices and removable devices and media, before reusing them or disposing of them.

- Create a separate user-level account for each person performing daily operation of a system. Use administrative-level accounts for system administration tasks only.

- In non-managed environments, create a password reset disk for the system and store it in a physically secure location.

- Disable and rename the built-in Administrator and Guest accounts.

- Use a password-enabled screen saver to protect the system from unauthorized local access.

- Review audit logs on a regular basis.

- Use Windows Firewall to restrict inbound network connections unless the system is already protected by a third-party host-based firewall.

- Use a stronger security solution than WEP whenever possible for wireless networking.

- Configure the system not to create dump files, unless they are specifically needed for troubleshooting purposes.

8. Application Security Configuration Recommendations

This section addresses security configuration for six types of applications that are commonly used on Windows XP systems: productivity application suites, e-mail clients, Web browsers, antivirus software, personal firewalls, and antivirus software.[136] Examples of security configuration tasks include telling an application to download updates automatically on a weekly basis, disabling unnecessary functionality, and enabling options that force users to approve certain actions, such as accepting a cookie in a Web browser. The purpose of this section is to highlight important elements of security configuration for each type of application; security configuration capabilities vary among products, so the recommendations provided in this section are not comprehensive, nor do they apply to every product.

Most of the security configuration recommendations in this section are specifically intended to provide protection against viruses, worms, Trojan horses, spyware, and other types of malware.[137] When configuring applications, administrators and users should also comply with local policy regarding the use of macros, mobile code (e.g., Java, JavaScript, ActiveX), browser plug-ins, and other types of code that may pose an increased security risk.

Organizations should carefully test application security settings before deploying them across an organization to ensure that they are sufficiently strong for the organization's needs and that they do not inadvertently interfere with other functionality.[138] Also, it is recommended to perform a system backup before installing or reconfiguring software, because these actions could modify system files, the Windows registry, or other critical system elements. It is important to maintain a functional backup copy of the system in case of an error. Section 4.2 includes information on performing system backups.

8.1 Productivity Application Suites

A *productivity application suite* refers to a set of integrated applications that provides several different types of functionality, such as word processing and spreadsheets. Typically, each application within the suite has a similar interface, and many features are provided by two or more applications in the suite. Recommendations for securing productivity application suites include:

- Ensure that all productivity application suites are kept current with patches and updates.

- Configure macro features so as to reduce the likelihood that they will be exploited for malware propagation. For example, some suites allow administrators to specify if macros can be run automatically or if the user has to consent to running each macro. Another feature offered by some suites is to specify from which directories macros may be run.

- Disable collaboration capabilities unless they are needed.

---

[136] The applications in this section are by no means a complete list of applications to install on Windows XP systems, nor does this guide imply any endorsement of certain products.

[137] For more information on malware, refer to NIST SP 800-83, *Guide to Malware Incident Prevention and Handling*, and NIST SP 800-28 Version 2, *Guidelines on Active Content and Mobile Code*, which are both available at http://csrc.nist.gov/publications/PubsSPs.html.

[138] Additional information on possible incompatibilities between applications and Windows XP SP2 or SP3 is available from Microsoft's Application Compatibility and User Account Control site at http://technet.microsoft.com/en-us/windows/aa905066.aspx.

8.2 Web Browsers

Since Web browsers are capable of parsing many forms of active code, including JavaScript, ActiveX, and Java, malicious individuals often take advantage of this to attack systems, distribute malware, or otherwise negatively impact systems. For example, certain types of cookies deposited on a user's system can be used to track the user's browsing habits and report them to an external server. Therefore, organizations should carefully consider the possible implications of enabling these functions. Recommendations for securing web browsers include:

- Ensure that all web browsers are kept current with patches and updates.

- Restrict active content and scripting, such as specifying which types of active content and scripts may be executed from which locations or types of locations (e.g., organization servers, external servers).

- Have the browser verify that each Web site's digital certificate has not been revoked before accepting it as legitimate and current.

- Restrict cookie handling; for example, prompt users to accept each third-party cookie that is presented to the system, and permit cookies only for the originating web site.

- Enable the browser's popup windows blocker, and specify any allowed sites in an exception list.

8.3 E-mail Clients

E-mail has become a primary means for business and personal communication, as well as malware propagation. Careful configuration of e-mail clients is important not only to protect a given computer, but also to prevent the propagation of viruses and worms from the computer to others. Securing e-mail applications involves using antivirus and antispyware software, raising user awareness of sound e-mail security practices, restricting privileges on e-mail attachment directories,[139] and properly configuring e-mail clients, including anti-spam mechanisms.[140] To operate an e-mail application in a secure manner, it is recommended that the software be patched regularly[141] and that the execution of active content be restricted or disabled entirely. Additional recommendations for e-mail client security include:

- Enable junk e-mail filtering capabilities.

- Set the default format for email message composition to plain text (not HTML, rich text, etc.)

- Disable the loading of remote images within e-mail messages. One of the benefits of enabling this setting is that it prevents spam messages from using small images within e-mails to track which users have opened them.

- Disable automatic opening of e-mail messages. Automatic opening can cause malicious contents to be executed without the user's involvement.

---

[139] Configuring e-mail attachment directories so that files in them cannot be executed (e.g., removing the Execute right from the directories) can prevent certain types of malicious attachments from being run on systems. A user would have to manually move such a file to an unprotected directory and then run it to infect the system. All users should be made aware of this and instructed on the accepted methods for handling attachments.

[140] Spam can negatively impact security in several ways. For example, some spam contains malicious content that could infect users' systems; other spam uses social engineering techniques to trick users into visiting phony Web sites or otherwise revealing sensitive information, such as social security numbers, credit card numbers, and passwords.

[141] In managed environments, updates should be performed consistent with local policy.

- Disable the automatic sending of return receipts.

8.4 Personal Firewalls

Personal firewalls provide restrictions on incoming network activity (and sometimes, outgoing activity as well) at a host level. Initially, personal firewalls were primarily used for hosts that were directly accessible from the Internet, but organizations are increasingly deploying personal firewalls to nearly all hosts to limit the spread of worms, among other reasons. Some personal firewalls can also restrict certain types of application activity, such as monitoring inbound and outbound e-mails for signs of malware and temporarily shutting off e-mail services if such activity is detected. Some personal firewalls also provide additional security for web browsers, such as suppressing popup windows and handling active code.

Because the capabilities of personal firewalls are so varied, organizations should carefully consider each product's capabilities when determining how to configure it. Additional information on personal firewall configuration is available from NIST SP 800-41 Revision 1 (Draft), *Guide to Firewalls and Firewall Policy*.[142] Also, Section 7.6 of this publication describes the Windows Firewall, a personal firewall provided with Windows XP Professional.

8.5 Antivirus Software

Antivirus software is an essential element of securing Windows XP systems, but it cannot provide full protection against all malware. Good computing practices should be followed even when antivirus software is installed, enabled, and fully updated. Examples of good practices are not opening unexpected file attachments and configuring applications not to execute macros or embedded HTML tags by default. Section 7.1.2 provides directions for mapping active content file extensions so that files are not automatically executed by default. Good practices also help to guard against the small time window between the release of a new virus and the availability of updated antivirus signatures.[143]

Although several brands of antivirus software are available, they offer similar functionality, as follows:

- Scanning critical system components such as startup files, system BIOS, and boot records

- Watching the real-time activities of the computer and operating system to check for suspicious activity; a common example is scanning all e-mail attachments for known viruses as e-mails are sent and received

- Scanning all files on a hard disk for known viruses. NIST recommends that antivirus software on Windows XP systems be configured to scan all hard drives regularly to identify any file system infections.

- Automatically downloading and installing updates from the vendor's Web site (or a local server in a managed environment) daily.

Each of these functions is important and should neither be ignored nor disabled unless necessary. Although the inherent risk behind virus scanning technology is that it primarily intercepts known viruses, this does not diminish the importance of the software. NIST strongly recommends that every Windows XP system use properly configured and maintained antivirus software. Antivirus software should be installed immediately after the initial Windows XP installation, and then updated with the newest

---

[142] http://csrc.nist.gov/publications/PubsDrafts.html
[143] For more information on antivirus software and malware, see NIST SP 800-83, *Guide to Malware Incident Prevention and Handling*, available at http://csrc.nist.gov/publications/PubsSPs.html.

signatures and antivirus software patches. The antivirus software should then perform a complete scan of the system to identify any potential infections.

Microsoft also offers a utility called the Windows Malicious Software Removal Tool. It checks for and attempts to remove certain common malware threats, such as worms and rootkits. The tool can be installed on systems automatically through Automatic Updates or Microsoft Update, or it can be downloaded or run directly from Microsoft's Web site.[144] Because the tool is designed to detect only a small number of common threats, it is a supplement to antivirus software, not a replacement.

8.6 Antispyware Software

Spyware refers to software and software components that collect information and use connectivity without the user's knowledge, typically to track users' behavior (e.g., Web sites visited) and report it to a central location. Examples of spyware include a standalone program installed on a user's system and a tracking cookie placed in a Web browser. Spyware not only violates users' privacy, but it can also cause functional problems on systems, such as slowing performance or causing application instabilities. Antispyware software has been created to identify many types of spyware on systems and quarantine or remove spyware files. Many antivirus software programs also offer some antispyware capabilities.

NIST recommends that every Windows XP system use either antispyware software or antivirus software with robust antispyware capabilities. The software should be installed immediately after the Windows XP installation and then updated with the newest signatures and other updates. The software should then perform a complete scan of the system to identify any potential infections. The software should also be configured to automatically download and install updates daily.

---

[144] The tool is available at http://www.microsoft.com/security/malwareremove/default.mspx. Additional information is available from MSKB article 890830, available at http://support.microsoft.com/?id=890830.

9. Putting It All Together

This publication covers many topics related to the security of Windows XP systems. The purpose of this section is to put it all together by describing the basic process that IT professionals should follow to use this publication and the accompanying templates. The primary steps are as follows:

1. Read the entire publication, including the appendices. As needed, review the additional reference material listed throughout the publication and in Appendix E.

2. As discussed in Section 4, install and patch the OS and applications on test systems, and create and test plans for system backups and restores.

3. Refer to Section 2 to review the system roles and threats, then select the appropriate operating environment. Review the security template or GPO corresponding to that environment. Refer to Section 6 as needed for more information on the different regions and values within the template.

4. Modify the template or GPO to reflect local policy and apply it to test systems using the appropriate deployment tool, as described in Section 5. Create multiple versions of the template or GPO if necessary to address multiple system roles or environments. Refer to Appendix D for other tools that may be useful for deployment.

5. Augment the template or GPO settings with additional controls presented in Section 7, as well as any others that are required based on the local environment. Also, apply application-specific security configuration changes, such as those described in Section 8.

6. Verify that the controls have been deployed properly by testing system functions and security controls, as described in Sections 2.5 and 4.4. Modify and document any changes made to the baseline security controls (e.g., altering a setting so a particular application can function properly). Modify the templates and GPOs as necessary to incorporate changes that apply to all systems.

7. Perform another round of testing in a test environment before deploying the templates or GPOs and other changes to production systems.

8. Deploy the templates or GPOs and additional controls to production systems. Verify that the controls have been deployed properly by testing system functions and security controls.

9. Maintain the systems, as described in Section 2.6. This includes keeping systems updated (Section 4.3), monitoring the system's primary security controls (Section 4.4), performing periodic vulnerability assessments (Section 4.4), and monitoring the various logs described throughout the publication.

Appendix A—Federal Agency Security Configurations

As discussed in Section 5, NIST collaborated with several other organizations to produce a set of Windows XP security templates corresponding to four environments—enterprise, SOHO, SSLF, and legacy. NIST has also made available GPOs for the FDCC specification settings.[145] The NIST templates and FDCC GPOs define similar security settings, including the following categories (listed as they appear in the Group Policy Editor[146]):

- Account policies: password policies and account security

- Local policies: system audit policy, user rights assignment, and security options

- Event log policies

- System services

- File permissions

There are a few differences in the types of settings the NIST templates and FDCC GPOs address. The templates define Restricted Groups settings, but the GPOs do not. Another important difference is that FDCC includes settings for Internet Explorer 7 (IE7) and Windows Firewall.

More information on the significance of many of the settings is available from Microsoft's *Threats and Countermeasures Guide: Security Settings in Windows Server 2003 and Windows XP*[147], from Section 6 of this document, and from a settings database created by NIST. The database, called the NIST Windows Security Baseline Database, contains information on all the settings from the NIST templates and the FDCC GPOs.[148] The database is self-contained so that it can be downloaded and run locally. It allows interested parties to view settings by baseline (e.g., Windows XP, IE7) or by policy (e.g., FDCC), as well as to compare baselines to each other, such as comparing the NIST enterprise template baseline with the FDCC baseline.

---

[145] More information on FDCC, including a spreadsheet containing a full list of all the FDCC settings, is available at http://nvd.nist.gov/fdcc/index.cfm.

[146] In an Active Directory managed environment, the following settings should be defined and applied at the domain level: Password Policy Settings; Account Lockout Policy Settings; "Add workstations to domain" setting in the User Rights Assignment policy; and "Microsoft network server: Disconnect clients when logon hours expire", "Network access: Allow anonymous SID/Name translation", and "Network security: Force logoff when logon hours expire" settings in the Security Options policy".

[147] http://www.microsoft.com/downloads/details.aspx?FamilyId=1B6ACF93-147A-4481-9346-F93A4081EEA8&displaylang=en

[148] The database contains a copy of the FDCC GPO information, and is not intended to become the official source of FDCC settings. The authoritative source of FDCC configuration information continues to be http://nvd.nist.gov/fdcc/index.cfm.

In addition to the actual baseline settings, each entry in the database contains other supporting data fields, including the Common Configuration Enumeration (CCE) identifier[149], the policy path and setting name, the description of the setting, and the object (such as a registry key path).

The database is freely available for download from http://csrc.nist.gov/itsec/guidance_WinXP.html.

---

[149] For more information on CCE, visit http://cce.mitre.org/.

Appendix B—Windows XP Service Pack 3 Security

Windows XP Service Pack 3 (SP3) was released to the public in May 2008.[150] It bundles many Windows XP security updates that were released since SP2 became available in 2004. SP3 also includes some Windows XP product features that were previously available only as individual downloads. Examples of these product features are:

- IPSec Simple Policy Update for Windows Server 2003 and Windows XP, which affects the development of IPSec filters

- Digital Identity Management Service (DIMS), which involves user access to digital certificates and private cryptographic keys

- Wi-Fi Protected Access 2 (WPA2), which is a wireless networking product certification. WPA2 is briefly mentioned in Section 7.8.

In terms of new or improved security functionality, SP3 offers few changes from SP2. The most notable changes include the following:

- Network Access Protection (NAP), which can be used to perform system health checks on Windows XP systems before allowing them to join a network or conduct other activities

- More detailed text in the Security Options control panel to better explain the significance of security settings

- Updated cryptographic modules. Windows XP SP3 supports SHA-256, SHA-384, and SHA-512 for X.509 certificate validation. Cryptographic modules in SP3 are also now FIPS-validated.

References to additional sources of information on Windows XP SP3 are available in Appendix F.

---

[150] All of the information presented in this appendix is derived from *Overview of Windows XP Service Pack 3* by Microsoft, which is available at http://download.microsoft.com/download/6/8/7/687484ed-8174-496d-8db9-f02b40c12982/Overview%20of%20Windows%20XP%20Service%20Pack%203.pdf.

Appendix C—Mapping Windows XP Controls to NIST SP 800-53

Appendix C maps many Windows XP security controls and security template settings referenced throughout this document to their corresponding NIST SP 800-53 Revision 2 controls. The list of controls and mapping is not intended to be fully comprehensive or authoritative, and it omits all SP 800-53 controls that are not directly related to individual Windows XP systems. The mappings are listed according to the control family categories established in SP 800-53. Each category has a separate table, with three columns containing the following information for each mapping:

- Number and name of the control from SP 800-53

- The sections of this publication that map to the SP 800-53 control, and a brief description of the content within those sections that corresponds to the SP 800-53 control

- The settings within Appendix A of this publication that map to the SP 800-53 control, if any.

The tables include the requirements and control enhancements that apply to low, moderate, and high impact systems. (Section 2.2 contains definitions for the impact categories). After determining the impact level of a system, administrators can select the SP 800-53 controls that correspond to that impact level, and then identify the sections of this document and template settings that match those SP 800-53 controls. This would provide a starting point for identifying all of the security controls needed to secure the system.

C.1 Management Controls

This section contains mappings for the following families of management controls:

- Certification, Accreditation, and Security Assessments (CA)

- Planning (PL)

- Risk Assessment (RA)

- System and Services Acquisition (SA).

Table C-1. Certification, Accreditation, and Security Assessments (CA) Family Controls

SP 800-53 Control Number and Name	Corresponding SP 800-68 Sections	Corresponding NIST Template Settings
CA-3: Information system connections	• Section 2.4.5 (Authorization to connect to network)	N/A
CA-7: Continuous monitoring	• Section 2.6 (Monitoring security controls and configuration changes) • Section 3.1.3 (Monitoring the status of common security controls)	N/A

Table C-2. Planning (PL) Family Controls

SP 800-53 Control Number and Name	Corresponding SP 800-68 Sections	Corresponding NIST Template Settings
PL-4: Rules of behavior	• Section 2.4.5 (Having a rules of behavior document)	N/A

Table C-3. Risk Assessment (RA) Family Controls

SP 800-53 Control Number and Name	Corresponding SP 800-68 Sections	Corresponding NIST Template Settings
RA-2: Security categorization	• Section 2.2 (Describes FIPS 199 security categories and their relationship to SP 800-53 controls)	N/A
RA-3: Risk assessment	• Section 2.3 (Defining threats, conducting risk assessments, performing risk mitigation)	N/A
RA-5: Vulnerability scanning	• Section 2.6 (Performing vulnerability assessments to assess the security posture of the system) • Section 4.4 (Using vulnerability scanners to identify security issues)	N/A

Table C-4. System and Services Acquisition (SA) Family Controls

SP 800-53 Control Number and Name	Corresponding SP 800-68 Sections	Corresponding NIST Template Settings
SA-5: Information system documentation	• Section 2.4.5 (Having a security configuration guide and other security-related documentation)	N/A
SA-7: User installed software	• Section 2.3.2.3 (Not installing or using non-approved applications) • Section 3.1.3 (Using software restriction policies to limit which software can be executed on a system) • Section 7.4 (Using software restriction policies to limit which software can be executed on a system)	N/A

C.2 Operational Controls

This section contains mappings for the following families of operational controls:

- Awareness and Training (AT)
- Configuration Management (CM)
- Contingency Planning (CP)
- Incident Response (IR)
- Maintenance (MA)
- Media Protection (MP)
- Personnel Security (PS)

- Physical and Environmental Protection (PE)
- System and Information Integrity (SI).

Table C-5. Awareness and Training (AT) Family Controls

SP 800-53 Control Number and Name	Corresponding SP 800-68 Sections	Corresponding NIST Template Settings
AT-2: Security awareness	• Section 2.3.2.3 (Educating users on avoiding malware infections) • Section 2.4.5 (Having security awareness and training for end users and administrators)	N/A
AT-3: Security training	• Section 2.4.5 (Having security awareness and training for end users and administrators)	N/A

Table C-6. Configuration Management (CM) Family Controls

SP 800-53 Control Number and Name	Corresponding SP 800-68 Sections	Corresponding NIST Template Settings
CM-1: Configuration management policy and procedures	• Section 2.4.5 (Having a configuration management policy, plan, and procedures) • Section 4 (Having a configuration management policy for operating system and application installation and changes)	N/A
CM-3: Configuration change control	• Section 2.5 (Documenting changes to default security templates and settings) • Section 2.6 (Logging all hardware maintenance activities)	N/A
CM-4: Monitoring configuration changes	• Section 2.5 (Testing changes to security controls) • Section 7 (Considering the effect each decision made regarding a system might have on its security) • Section 5.3 (Determine the effect of applying security templates for a particular user or computer)	N/A
CM-6: Configuration settings	• Section 2.4.5 (Having a security configuration guide) • Section 5 (Using security templates to set security-relevant system settings) • Section 5.1 (Using security templates to compare actual settings to required settings) • Section 5.2 (Using security templates to compare actual settings to required settings)	All
CM-7: Least functionality	• Section 2.3.1.3 (Disabling unused local services)	N/A
	• Section 2.3.2.1 (Disabling unused network services)	N/A
	• Section 4.1.2.1 (Disabling unneeded network clients, services, and protocols; removing unneeded applications and utilities)	N/A
	• Section 6.2.3 (Restricting the performance of certain actions)	Security Options settings
	• Section 6.5 (Disabling unnecessary services)	System Services settings

SP 800-53 Control Number and Name	Corresponding SP 800-68 Sections	Corresponding NIST Template Settings
	• Section 6.8.2 (Removing filtering exemptions for Kerberos and RSVP traffic)	Setting 5.79
	• Section 6.8.4 (Disabling Dr. Watson feature)	N/A
	• Section 7.5 (Using only the necessary network protocols and components)	N/A
	• Section 7.6 (Using Windows Firewall to block access to ports)	
	• Section 7.7 (Removing filtering exemptions for Kerberos and RSVP traffic)	Setting 5.79
	• Section 7.7 (Using IPsec filters to restrict network traffic)	N/A

Table C-7. Contingency Planning (CP) Family Controls

SP 800-53 Control Number and Name	Corresponding SP 800-68 Sections	Corresponding NIST Template Settings
CP-2: Contingency plan	• Section 2.3 (Performing contingency planning) • Section 2.4.5 (Having IT contingency plans)	N/A
CP-9: Information system backup	• Section 2.3 (Performing backups, storing them in a safe and secure location, and testing them regularly) • Section 4.2 (Performing backups and restores; testing backups)	N/A

Table C-8. Incident Response (IR) Family Controls

SP 800-53 Control Number and Name	Corresponding SP 800-68 Sections	Corresponding NIST Template Settings
IR-1: Incident response policy and procedures	• Section 2.6 (Having an organization incident response policy)	N/A
IR-4: Incident handling	• Section 2.6 (Having a formal incident response capability)	N/A

Table C-9. Maintenance (MA) Family Controls

SP 800-53 Control Number and Name	Corresponding SP 800-68 Sections	Corresponding NIST Template Settings
MA-1: System maintenance policy and procedures	• Section 2.3.2.3 (Creating a plan for maintaining Windows XP systems)	N/A
MA-2: Controlled maintenance	• Section 2.6 (Performs regular security maintenance)	N/A
MA-4: Remote maintenance	• Section 2.6 (Providing remote system administration and assistance)	N/A

Table C-10. Media Protection (MP) Family Controls

SP 800-53 Control Number and Name	Corresponding SP 800-68 Sections	Corresponding NIST Template Settings
MP-4: Media storage	• Section 2.3.1.2 (Physically securing removable media) • Section 2.6 (Protecting media) • Section 4.1.2.2 (Physically securing image media) • Section 4.2 (Storing and protecting backup media) • Section 7.2.5 (Protecting password reset disks)	N/A
MP-6: Media sanitization and disposal	• Section 2.6 (Sanitizing media) • Section 7.1.5 (Sanitizing all fixed and removable storage media, destroying storage devices)	N/A

Table C-11. Personnel Security (PS) Family Controls

SP 800-53 Control Number and Name	Corresponding SP 800-68 Sections	Corresponding NIST Template Settings
PS-4: Personnel termination	• Section 2.3.1.2 (Disabling accounts as soon as employees leave the organization) • Section 2.3.2.1 (Disabling accounts as soon as employees leave the organization) • Section 7.2.1 (Disabling accounts as soon as they are no longer needed, such as an employee leaving the organization)	N/A
PS-5: Personnel transfer	• Section 7.2.1 (Disabling accounts as soon as they are no longer needed, such as an employee whose responsibilities change)	N/A

Table C-12. Physical and Environmental Protection (PE) Family Controls

SP 800-53 Control Number and Name	Corresponding SP 800-68 Sections	Corresponding NIST Template Settings
PE-1: Physical and environmental protection policy and procedures	• Section 2.3.1.1 (Having a physical and environmental protection policy)	N/A
PE-3: Physical access control	• Section 2.3.1.1 (Implementing physical securing measures to restrict access to systems) • Section 2.3.2.3 (Restricting physical access to systems)	N/A
PE-11: Emergency power	• Section 4.2 (Using a UPS to provide temporary emergency battery power)	N/A

Table C-13. System and Information Integrity (SI) Family Controls

SP 800-53 Control Number and Name	Corresponding SP 800-68 Sections	Corresponding NIST Template Settings
SI-2: Flaw remediation	<ul><li>Section 2.3.1.3 (Installing application and OS updates)</li><li>Section 2.3.2.1 (Testing and installing application and OS updates)</li><li>Section 2.6 (Acquiring and installing software updates)</li><li>Section 4.3 (Acquiring and installing security updates)</li><li>Section 4.3.5 (Performing patching in managed environments)</li><li>Section 4.4 (Checking the patch status of computers)</li></ul>	N/A
SI-3: Malicious code protection	<ul><li>Section 2.3.2.3 (Protecting systems from malicious payloads; using antivirus and antispyware software; configuring server and client software to reduce exposure to malware)</li><li>Section 3.1.3 (Using the Data Execution Prevention feature to stop attacks using buffer overflows)</li><li>Section 7.1.2 (Changing default file associations used by malware; displaying full filenames to identify suspicious extensions used by malware)</li><li>Section 7.1.3 (Displaying full filenames to identify suspicious extensions used by malware)</li></ul>	N/A
SI-4: Information system monitoring tools and techniques	<ul><li>Section 2.6 (Monitoring event logs to identify problems and suspicious activity)</li><li>Section 8.4 (Using personal firewalls to block outbound communications from malware)</li></ul>	N/A
SI-5: Security alerts and advisories	<ul><li>Section 2.3.2.3 (Monitoring Microsoft mailing lists for relevant security bulletins)</li><li>Section 2.6 (Subscribing to and monitoring vulnerability notification mailing lists)</li></ul>	N/A
SI-6: Security functionality verification	<ul><li>Section 3.1.3 (Having Windows Security Center identify and report failures or major misconfigurations of certain security controls)</li><li>Section 4.4 (Having Windows Security Center identify and report failures or major misconfigurations of certain security controls; performing central monitoring of security controls)</li></ul>	N/A
SI-7: Software and information integrity	<ul><li>Section 2.6 (Monitoring changes to OS and software settings)</li><li>Section 3.1.3 (Using software restriction policies to prevent unwanted executables from running)</li><li>Section 7.4 (Using software restriction policies to prevent unwanted executables from running)</li></ul>	N/A

SP 800-53 Control Number and Name	Corresponding SP 800-68 Sections	Corresponding NIST Template Settings
SI-8: Spam protection	• Section 2.3.2.3 (Protecting systems from malicious payloads; using e-mail clients that support spam filtering) • Section 8.3 (Configuring e-mail clients to use anti-spam features; configuring e-mail clients not to load remote images automatically, which could be spyware) • Section 8.4 (Using personal firewalls to limit Web browser cookies, including spyware tracking cookies) • Section 8.6 (Using and updating antispyware software)	N/A

C.3 Technical Controls

This section contains mappings for the following families of technical controls:

- Access Control (AC)
- Audit and Accountability (AU)
- Identification and Authentication (IA)
- System and Communications Protection (SC).

Table C-14. Access Control (AC) Family Controls

SP 800-53 Control Number and Name	Corresponding SP 800-68 Sections	Corresponding NIST Template Settings
AC-2: Account management	• Section 7.2.1 (Disabling inactive, unneeded, and temporary accounts; deleting disabled accounts)	N/A
AC-3: Access enforcement	• Section 2.3.1.1 (Encrypting local files to prevent access) • Section 2.3.1.3 (Encrypting sensitive data) • Section 3.1.2 (Protecting personal data and settings through the use of individual user accounts; limiting remote access to user accounts and shares) • Section 3.2.5 (Encrypting local files to prevent access) • Section 6.2.2 (Having users belong to only the necessary groups)	N/A
	• Section 6.2.2 (Giving only the necessary rights to groups)	User Rights Assignment settings
	• Section 6.2.3 (Setting security options to restrict the actions that users can perform)	Security Options settings
	• Section 6.4 (Limiting membership in groups with certain privileges)	Restricted Groups settings
	• Section 6.6 (Setting file permissions)	File Permission settings

SP 800-53 Control Number and Name	Corresponding SP 800-68 Sections	Corresponding NIST Template Settings
	• Section 6.7 (Setting registry permissions) • Section 7.1.1 (Using the NTFS filesystem) • Section 7.1.4 (Encrypting local files to prevent access)	N/A
AC-4: Information flow enforcement	• Section 2.3.2.1 (Using a firewall to limit network access to a host) • Section 3.1.1 (Using a personal firewall to restrict network traffic) • Section 7.5 (Securing network interfaces and disabling unneeded networking components) • Section 7.6 (Using a personal firewall to restrict network traffic)	N/A
AC-6: Least privilege	• Section 2.2 (Assigning user rights based on least privilege) • Section 6.2.2 (Assigning user rights based on least privilege)	N/A
AC-7: Unsuccessful login attempts	• Section 6.1 (Locking out accounts after too many failed login attempts)	Settings 2.1 (Lockout duration), 2.2 (Lockout threshold), and 2.3 (Reset counter after x minutes)
AC-8: System use notification	• Section 2.3.1.2 (Presenting a warning banner when a user attempts to log on) • Section 2.3.2.1 (Presenting a warning banner when a user attempts to log on)	Settings 5.29 (Banner message text) and 5.30 (Banner message title)
AC-11: Session lock	• Section 2.3.1.2 (Using a password-protected screen saver) • Section 7.2.4 (Using a password-protected screen saver, manually locking user sessions)	N/A
AC-17: Remote access	• Section 2.3.2.1 (Using industry-standard strong protocols for remote access) • Section 3.1.1 (Disabling built-in remote access services that are not needed)	N/A
	• Section 6.4 (Limiting membership in the Remote Desktop Users group)	Setting 7.3
	• Section 6.5 (Disabling the Remote Assistance and Remote Desktop services)	N/A
AC-18: Wireless access restrictions	• Section 3.1.1 (Not connecting to any wireless network automatically, using wireless security features) • Section 7.8 (Using wireless security features)	N/A

Table C-15. Audit and Accountability (AU) Family Controls

SP 800-53 Control Number and Name	Corresponding SP 800-68 Sections	Corresponding NIST Template Settings
AU-2: Auditable events	• Section 6.2.1 (Configuring system auditing)	Audit Policy settings
	• Section 7.3.1 (Auditing access to particular files)	N/A

SP 800-53 Control Number and Name	Corresponding SP 800-68 Sections	Corresponding NIST Template Settings
AU-4: Audit storage capacity	• Section 6.3 (Enabling logging and specifying maximum log sizes)	Event Log Policy settings
AU-6: Audit monitoring, analysis, and reporting	• Section 2.6 (Monitoring logs) • Section 7.3.2 (Reviewing logs)	N/A
AU-8: Time stamps	• Section 7.3.3 (Performing clock synchronization)	N/A

Table C-16. Identification and Authentication (IA) Family Controls

SP 800-53 Control Number and Name	Corresponding SP 800-68 Sections	Corresponding NIST Template Settings
IA-1: Identification and authentication policy and procedures	• Section 2.3.1.2 (Having a password policy) • Section 2.3.2.1 (Having a password policy)	N/A
IA-2: User identification and authentication	• Section 2.3.1.2 (Requiring valid username and password authentication) • Section 2.3.1.3 (Requiring strong passwords for administrator accounts) • Section 2.3.2.1 (Requiring strong authentication for using network services) • Section 2.3.2.3 (Using a daily use account for normal system operations; using an administrator-level account only when needed for specific tasks) • Section 3.1.2 (Having an individual user account for each person) • Section 3.2.1 (Using Kerberos for authentication) • Section 3.2.2 (Using smart cards for authentication)	N/A
	• Section 6.8.1 (Not permitting system login to be bypassed)	Setting 5.70
	• Section 7.2 (Disabling default accounts, creating a separate daily use account for each user)	N/A
IA-4: Identifier management	• Section 6.1 (Having strong passwords for each user account) • Section 7.2 (Creating a separate daily use account for each user)	N/A
IA-5: Authenticator management	• Section 2.3.2.2 (Using a secure user identification and authentication system) • Section 3.1.2 (Preventing null or blank passwords for network login and the secondary logon service; storing authentication information for operating systems and applications) • Section 4.1.2.1 (Setting strong passwords for new accounts) • Section 6.1 (Using a secure user identification and authentication system)	N/A
	• Section 6.1 (Setting minimum and maximum password ages; preventing password reuse through password history; storing encrypted passwords)	Password Policy settings

Table C-17. System and Communications Protection (SC) Family Controls

SP 800-53 Control Number and Name	Corresponding SP 800-68 Sections	Corresponding NIST Template Settings
SC-4: Information remnants	• Section 6.8.4 (Disabling the creation of memory dump files) • Section 7.9 (Disabling the creation of memory dump files; clearing page files at system shutdown; disabling the use of hibernation files)	N/A
SC-5: Denial of service protection	• Section 6.8.2 (Configuring networking settings to prevent or limit certain denial of service attacks)	Security Options settings
SC-8: Transmission integrity	• Section 3.2.4 (Using IPsec to protect network communications) • Section 7.7 (Using IPsec to protect network communications)	N/A
SC-9: Transmission confidentiality	• Section 2.3.2.2 (Encrypting network communications) • Section 3.2.4 (Using IPsec to protect network communications) • Section 7.7 (Using IPsec to protect network communications)	N/A
SC-13: Use of cryptography	• Section 7.8 (Using FIPS-approved encryption algorithms)	N/A
SC-18: Mobile code	• Section 2.3.2.3 (Configuring systems so that default file associations prevent automatic execution of active content files)	N/A

Appendix D—Commonly Used TCP/IP Ports on Windows XP Systems

Appendix D lists commonly used TCP/IP ports on Windows XP systems.[151]

Table D-1. Commonly Used TCP/IP Ports

Port	Protocol	Service	Description
21	TCP	FTP	File Transfer Protocol server
23	TCP	Telnet	Telnet service
68	UDP	DHCP	Dynamic Host Configuration Protocol client
80	TCP	HTTP	HyperText Transfer Protocol server
123	UDP	NTP	Network Time Protocol client (Windows Time)
135	TCP	epmap	DCE Endpoint Resolution (remote procedure call)
137	UDP	NetBIOS-ns	NetBIOS Name Service
138	UDP	NetBIOS-dgm	NetBIOS Datagram Service
139	TCP	NetBIOS-ssn	NetBIOS Session Service
161	UDP	SNMP	Simple Network Management Protocol
213	UDP	IPX Over IP	Client Service for Netware service
443	TCP	HTTPS	HTTP over SSL server
445	TCP, UDP	microsoft-ds (SMB)	Microsoft Common Internet File System (CIFS)
500	UDP	IKE	Internet Key Exchange (often used with IPsec)
515	TCP	LPR	Print Spooler service
522	TCP		NetMeeting client[152]
1503	TCP		NetMeeting client
1701	UDP	L2TP	Layer 2 Tunneling Protocol client
1720	TCP		NetMeeting client
1723	TCP/UDP	PPTP	Point-to-Point Tunneling Protocol client
1731	TCP		NetMeeting client
1900	UDP	SSDP	Simple Service Discovery Protocol
2001-2120	UDP		Windows Messenger voice calls[153]
2869	TCP	UPnP	Universal Plug and Play
3002	TCP		Windows Firewall/Sharing
3003	TCP		Windows Firewall/Sharing
3389	TCP	RDP	Remote Desktop Protocol service
4500	UDP	L2TP/IPsec	NAT-T L2TP/IPSec

---

[151] For more information on the ports used by Windows XP services, see the article titled *Windows Server 2003 System Services Reference*, available at http://www.microsoft.com/downloads/details.aspx?FamilyID=b38a0682-2997-4678-9d9e-a07cc66a3bba&displaylang=en, and MSKB article 832017, *Service overview and network port requirements for the Windows Server system*, at http://support.microsoft.com/?id=832017. Also, MSKB article 308127, *How to manually open ports in Internet Connection Firewall in Windows XP*, contains information on some native Windows XP ports, as well as ports used by various third-party software. This article is available at http://support.microsoft.com/?id=308127.

[152] Additional information on NetMeeting ports is available from Microsoft Technet at http://www.microsoft.com/technet/security/secnews/asktheexperts/ask2.mspx.

[153] More information on Windows Messenger ports is available from Barb Bowman's article, *Don't Let the Defense Rest*, available at http://www.microsoft.com/windowsxp/using/networking/expert/bowman_november12.mspx.

Port	Protocol	Service	Description
5000	TCP	UPnP	Universal Plug and Play
6801	UDP		Windows Messenger voice calls
6891-6900	TCP		Windows Messenger file transfers
6901	TCP/UDP		Windows Messenger voice calls

Appendix E—Tools

Appendix E summarizes various tools mentioned in this document that can be used to configure, manage, and monitor Windows XP security settings.

Table E-1. Windows XP Tools

Tool Name	Relevance	Reference
Automatic Updates	Checks Microsoft update server for new updates; downloads and installs them	Included with Windows XP
Cipher	Scrubs data from unused portions of disks	cipher.exe Included with Windows XP
Enterprise Scan Tool	Scans computers to identify particular security issues not detectable by MBSA	http://support.microsoft.com/?id=894193
Event Viewer	Displays application, security, and system log entries	eventvwr.exe Included with Windows XP
Group Policy Management Console (GPMC) MMC snap-in	Manages Group Policy for multiple domains	http://www.microsoft.com/windowsserver2003/gpmc/default.mspx
Group Policy Modeling Wizard MMC snap-in	Determines the effects of applying combinations of GPOs to a particular user or computer	http://www.microsoft.com/windowsserver2003/gpmc/default.mspx
Group Policy Object Editor MMC snap-in	Imports security template into a GPO	Included with Windows XP
Local Security Policy	Displays local security settings and allows administrator to alter settings	Included with Windows XP (Control Panel / Administrative Tools)
Microsoft Baseline Security Analyzer (MBSA)	Scans computers to identify security issues	http://technet.microsoft.com/en-us/security/cc184924.aspx
Microsoft Management Console	Acts as a container for snap-ins	mmc.exe Included with Windows XP
Microsoft Update	Checks for available updates, transfers them to system, and installs them	http://update.microsoft.com/
Port Reporter	Logs information on TCP and UDP port usage	http://www.microsoft.com/downloads/details.aspx?amp;displaylang=en&familyid=69BA779B-BAE9-4243-B9D6-63E62B4BCD2E&displaylang=en
Qchain.exe	Allows multiple hotfixes to be installed at one time	http://www.microsoft.com/downloads/details.aspx?amp;displaylang=en&familyid=3C64D889-74F1-490B-A2FB-F15671A3B60C&displaylang=en
Qfecheck.exe	Track and verify installed hotfixes	http://www.microsoft.com/downloads/details.aspx?displaylang=en&FamilyID=155C7C58-102E-47B0-A12A-BFAB8CFCCC03
Registry Editor	Provides a way for administrators to graphically view and edit registry entries	regedit.exe and regedt32.exe Included with Windows XP
Remote Installation Services	Allows Windows XP to be installed automatically on remote systems	Included with Windows 2000 and Windows 2003
Security Configuration and Analysis MMC snap-in	Compares the system's current security settings to the settings in a template	Included with Windows XP

Tool Name	Relevance	Reference
Security Templates MMC snap-in	Allows administrator to review, modify, and apply security templates	Included with Windows XP
Sysprep	Clones XP image onto other systems	sysprep.exe Included with Windows XP
Windows Malicious Software Removal Tool	Checks for and attempts to remove certain common malware threats	Installed automatically through Automatic Updates and Microsoft Update Can be downloaded or run directly from http://www.microsoft.com/security/malwareremove/default.mspx

Appendix F—Resources

F.1 Vulnerability Databases

- National Vulnerability Database (NVD)
  http://nvd.nist.gov/

- Open Source Vulnerability Database
  http://www.osvdb.org/

- SecurityFocus Vulnerability Database
  http://www.securityfocus.com/bid/

- United States Computer Emergency Readiness Team (US-CERT) Vulnerability Notes Database
  http://www.kb.cert.org/vuls/

F.2 Mailing Lists

- Microsoft Security Notification Service
  http://www.microsoft.com/technet/security/bulletin/notify.mspx

- SecurityFocus – BugTraq
  http://www.securityfocus.com/archive/1

- US-CERT National Cyber Alert System
  http://www.us-cert.gov/cas/

F.3 Print Resources

Allen, Robbie and Gralla, Preston, *Windows XP Cookbook*, O'Reilly, 2005.

Bott, Ed, et al., *Microsoft Windows XP Inside Out, Second Edition*, Microsoft Press, 2004.

Bott, Ed and Siechert, Carl, *Microsoft Windows Security Inside Out for Windows XP and Windows 2000*, Microsoft Press, 2002.

Boyce, Jim, *Windows XP Power Tools*, Sybex, 2002.

Honeycutt, Jerry, *Microsoft Windows XP Registry Guide*, Microsoft Press, 2002.

Moskowitz, Jeremy, *Group Policy, Profiles, and IntelliMirror for Windows 2003, Windows XP, and Windows 2000*, Sybex, 2004.

Moulton, Pete, *SOHO Networking: A Guide to Installing a Small-Office/Home-Office Network*, Prentice Hall PTR, 2002.

Russel, Charlie and Crawford, Sharon, *Microsoft Windows XP Professional Resource Kit, Third Edition*, Microsoft Press, 2005.

Simmons, Curt and Causey, James, *Microsoft Windows XP Networking Inside Out*, Microsoft Press, 2002.

Thurrott, Paul, *Windows XP Home Networking, 2nd Edition*, John Wiley and Sons, 2004.

Weber, Chris and Bahadur, Gary, *Windows XP Professional Security*, McGraw-Hill, 2002.

F.4 Related NIST Documents and Resources

- Computer Security Resource Center Special Publications
  http://csrc.nist.gov/publications/PubsSPs.html

    - SP 800-28 Version 2, *Guidelines on Active Content and Mobile Code*

    - SP 800-30, *Risk Management Guide for Information Technology Systems*

    - SP 800-34, *Contingency Planning Guide for Information Technology Systems*

    - SP 800-40 Version 2.0, *Procedures for Handling Security Patches*

    - SP 800-43, *Systems Administration Guidance for Securing Microsoft Windows 2000 Professional System*

    - SP 800-46, *Security for Telecommuting and Broadband Communications*

    - SP 800-48 Revision 1, *Guide to Securing Legacy IEEE Wireless Networks*

    - SP 800-53 Revision 2, *Recommended Security Controls for Federal Information Systems*

    - SP 800-61 Revision 1, *Computer Security Incident Handling Guide*

    - SP 800-63, *Electronic Authentication Guideline*

    - SP 800-70, *Security Configuration Checklists Program for IT Products*

    - SP 800-70 Revision 1 (Draft), *National Checklist Program for IT Products*

    - SP 800-77, *Guide to IPsec VPNs*

    - SP 800-83, *Guide to Malware Incident Prevention and Handling*

    - SP 800-88, *Guidelines for Media Sanitization*

    - SP 800-92, *Guide to Computer Security Log Management*

    - SP 800-97, *Establishing Wireless Robust Security Networks: A Guide to IEEE 802.11i*

    - SP 800-111, *Guide to Storage Encryption Technologies for End User Devices*

    - SP 800-115, *Technical Guide to Information Security Testing and Assessment*

- FIPS Publications
  http://csrc.nist.gov/publications/PubsFIPS.html

  - FIPS 140-2, *Security Requirements for Cryptographic Modules*

  - FIPS 199, *Standards for Security Categorization of Federal Information and Information Systems*

  - FIPS 200, *Minimum Security Requirements for Federal Information and Information Systems*

- FISMA Implementation Project
  http://csrc.nist.gov/groups/SMA/fisma/index.html

- National Checklist Program and Checklist Repository
  http://checklists.nist.gov/

- Security Content Automation Protocol (SCAP)
  http://nvd.nist.gov/scap.cfm

F.5 Microsoft Web-Based Resources

Microsoft's Web site contains a wealth of information regarding Windows XP and Windows security. This section lists many of these resources, divided into six categories: general Windows XP resources, general security resources (i.e., not XP-specific), general and specific Windows XP security resources, Microsoft knowledge base articles, and Windows XP SP3-specific resources.

F.5.1 General Windows XP Resources

- Microsoft Technet
  http://technet.microsoft.com/en-us/default.aspx

- Microsoft Windows XP Professional Resource Kit Documentation
  http://technet.microsoft.com/en-us/library/bb968968.aspx

- Windows Application Compatibility and User Account Control
  http://technet.microsoft.com/en-us/windows/aa905066.aspx

- Windows XP Home Page
  http://www.microsoft.com/windows/windows-xp/default.aspx

- Windows XP Professional Features
  http://technet.microsoft.com/en-us/library/bb457058(TechNet.10).aspx

- Windows XP Service Pack 2 – Step by Step
  http://support.microsoft.com/kb/889735/EN-US/

- *Administering Group Policy with Group Policy Management Console*
  http://technet2.microsoft.com/WindowsServer/f/?en/library/b9cb929b-4c2f-4754-ad31-d154bb8105771033.mspx

- *Enterprise Management with the Group Policy Management Console*
  http://www.microsoft.com/windowsserver2003/gpmc/default.mspx

F.5.2 General Security Resources

- Microsoft Download Center
  http://www.microsoft.com/downloads/search.aspx?displaylang=en

- Microsoft Security Central
  http://www.microsoft.com/security/

- Microsoft TechNet Security TechCenter
  http://technet.microsoft.com/en-us/security/default.aspx

- Microsoft Technical Security Notifications
  http://www.microsoft.com/technet/security/bulletin/notify.mspx

- Microsoft Windows Update Web site
  http://windowsupdate.microsoft.com/

- Security Bulletins
  http://signup.alerts.live.com/brochure/index.jsp

- Windows Server Update Services
  http://technet.microsoft.com/en-us/wsus/default.aspx

F.5.3 General Windows XP Security Resources

- *Group Policy Settings Reference for Windows Server 2003 with Service Pack 1*
  http://www.microsoft.com/downloads/details.aspx?FamilyID=7821c32f-da15-438d-8e48-45915cd2bc14&displaylang=en

- *Home and Small Office Network Topologies*
  http://technet.microsoft.com/en-us/library/bb457037.aspx

- *Securing Mobile Computers with Windows XP Professional*
  http://technet.microsoft.com/en-us/library/bb457043.aspx

- *Step-by-Step Guide to Securing Microsoft Windows XP Professional with Service Pack 2 in Small and Medium Businesses*
  http://www.microsoft.com/windowsxp/using/security/learnmore/smbsecurity.mspx

- *Threats and Countermeasures Guide: Security Settings in Windows Server 2003 and Windows XP*
  http://www.microsoft.com/downloads/details.aspx?FamilyId=1B6ACF93-147A-4481-9346-F93A4081EEA8&displaylang=en

- *What's New in Security for Windows XP Professional and Windows XP Home Edition*
  http://technet.microsoft.com/en-us/library/bb457059.aspx

- *Windows XP Baseline Security Checklists*
  http://www.microsoft.com/technet/archive/security/chklist/xpcl.mspx?mfr=true

- *Windows XP Security Guide v2.2*
  http://www.microsoft.com/downloads/details.aspx?familyid=2D3E25BC-F434-4CC6-A5A7-09A8A229F118&displaylang=en

- *Windows XP Service Pack 2 (SP2) Solution Center*
  http://support.microsoft.com/ph/6794

F.5.4 Specific Windows XP Security Topics

- *Configuring Windows XP IEEE 802.11 Wireless Networks for the Home and Small Business*
  http://www.microsoft.com/technet/network/wifi/wifisoho.mspx

- *Data Protection and Recovery in Windows XP*
  http://technet.microsoft.com/en-us/library/bb457020.aspx

- *Don't Let the Defense Rest: Securing Home Networks with Windows XP*
  http://www.microsoft.com/windowsxp/using/networking/expert/bowman_november12.mspx

- *Encrypting File System in Windows XP and Windows Server 2003*
  http://technet.microsoft.com/en-us/library/bb457065.aspx

- *Get Started Using Remote Desktop with Windows XP Professional*
  http://www.microsoft.com/windowsxp/using/mobility/getstarted/remoteintro.mspx

- *Guide for Installing and Deploying Updates for Microsoft Windows XP Service Pack 2*
  http://technet.microsoft.com/en-us/library/bb457071.aspx

- *How NTFS Works*
  http://technet.microsoft.com/en-us/library/cc781134.aspx

- *How to Set Up and Use Automated System Recovery in Windows XP*
  http://technet.microsoft.com/en-us/library/bb456980.aspx

- *How to Share Files Using Encrypting File System*
  http://www.microsoft.com/windowsxp/using/security/expert/sharefilesefs.mspx

- *How to Use Sysprep: An Introduction*
  http://technet.microsoft.com/en-us/library/bb457073.aspx

- *Manage Your Computer's Security Settings in One Place*
  http://www.microsoft.com/windowsxp/using/security/internet/sp2_wscintro.mspx

- *NTFS vs. FAT: Which Is Right for You?*
  http://www.microsoft.com/windowsxp/using/setup/expert/russel_october01.mspx

- *Predefined Security Templates*
  http://technet.microsoft.com/en-us/library/cc787720.aspx

- *Remote Installation Services*
  http://technet.microsoft.com/en-us/library/cc786442.aspx

- *Securing Wireless LANs with Certificate Services*
  http://www.microsoft.com/technet/security/prodtech/windowsserver2003/pkiwire/swlan.mspx?mfr=true

- *Securing Wireless LANs with PEAP and Passwords*
  http://www.microsoft.com/downloads/details.aspx?FamilyID=60c5d0a1-9820-480e-aa38-63485eca8b9b&displaylang=en

- *Set Up a Wired Network*
  http://www.microsoft.com/windowsxp/using/networking/setup/wired.mspx

- *Step-by-Step Guide to Internet Protocol Security (IPSec)*
  http://technet.microsoft.com/en-us/library/bb742429.aspx

- *Stored User Names and Passwords Overview*
  http://technet.microsoft.com/en-us/library/cc786845.aspx

- *Universal Plug and Play in Windows XP*
  http://technet.microsoft.com/en-us/library/bb457049.aspx

- *Using Software Restriction Policies to Protect Against Unauthorized Software*
  http://technet.microsoft.com/en-us/library/bb457006.aspx

- *Wireless Networking*
  http://technet.microsoft.com/en-us/network/bb530679.aspx

- *Windows Server 2003 System Services Reference*
  http://www.microsoft.com/downloads/details.aspx?FamilyID=b38a0682-2997-4678-9d9e-a07cc66a3bba&displaylang=en

- *Wireless Deployment Technology and Component Overview*
  http://technet.microsoft.com/en-us/library/bb457015.aspx

- *The Wireless XP Wireless Zero Configuration Service: The Cable Guy, November 2002*
  http://technet.microsoft.com/en-us/library/bb878124.aspx

F.5.5 Knowledge Base Articles

- Article 143475, *Windows NT System Key Permits Strong Encryption of the SAM*
  http://support.microsoft.com/?id=143475

- Article 217098, *Basic Overview of Kerberos User Authentication Protocol in Windows 2000*
  http://support.microsoft.com/?id=217098

- Article 243330, *Well-known security identifiers in Windows operating systems*
  http://support.microsoft.com/?id=243330

- Article 254649, *Overview of memory dump file options for Windows Server 2003, Windows XP, and Windows 2000*
  http://support.microsoft.com/?id=254649

- Article 279765, *How to Use the Fast User Switching Feature in Windows XP*
  http://support.microsoft.com/?id=279765

- Article 282784, *Qfecheck.exe verifies the installation of Windows 2000 and Windows XP hotfixes*
  http://support.microsoft.com/?id=282784

- Article 294739, *A discussion about the availability of the Fast User Switching feature*
  http://support.microsoft.com/?id=294739

- Article 296861, *How to install multiple Windows updates or hotfixes with only one reboot*
  http://support.microsoft.com/?id=296861

- Article 304040, *How to configure file sharing in Windows XP*
  http://support.microsoft.com/?id=304040

- Article 307973, *How to configure system failure and recovery options in Windows*
  http://support.microsoft.com/?id=307973

- Article 308422, *How to use the Backup utility that is included in Windows XP to back up files and folders*
  http://support.microsoft.com/?id=308422

- Article 309340, *How to use Backup to protect data and restore files and folders on your computer in Windows XP and Windows Vista*
  http://support.microsoft.com/?id=309340

- Article 310749, *New Capabilities and Features of the NTFS 3.1 File System*
  http://support.microsoft.com/?id=310749

- Article 314343, *Basic Storage Versus Dynamic Storage in Windows XP*
  http://support.microsoft.com/?id=314343

- Article 314834, *How to Clear the Windows Paging File at Shutdown*
  http://support.microsoft.com/?id=314834

- Article 314984, *How to create and delete hidden or administrative shares on client computers*
  http://support.microsoft.com/?id=314984

- Article 320820, *How to Use the Backup utility to back up files and folders in Windows XP Home Edition*
  http://support.microsoft.com/?id=320820

- Article 322389, *How to obtain the latest Windows XP service pack*
  http://support.microsoft.com/?id=322389

- Article 330904, *Messenger Service window that contains an Internet advertisement appears*
  http://support.microsoft.com/?id=330904

- Article 810207, *IPSec default exemptions are removed in Windows Server 2003*
  http://support.microsoft.com/?id=810207

- Article 837243, *Availability and description of the Port Reporter tool*
  http://support.microsoft.com/?id=837243

- Article 832017, *Service overview and network port requirements for the Windows Server system*
  http://support.microsoft.com/?id=832017

- Article 875352, *A detailed description of the Data Execution Prevention (DEP) feature in Windows XP Service Pack 2, Windows XP Tablet PC Edition 2005, and Windows Server 2003*
  http://support.microsoft.com/?id=875352

- Article 890830, *The Microsoft Windows Malicious Software Removal Tool helps remove specific prevalent malicious software from computers that are running Windows Vista, Windows Server 2003, Windows XP, or Windows 2000*
  http://support.microsoft.com/?id=890830

- Article 893357, *The Wi-Fi Protected Access 2 (WPA2)/Wireless Provisioning Services Information Element (WPS IE) update for Windows XP with Service Pack 2 is available*
  http://support.microsoft.com/?id=893357

- Article 894193, *How to obtain and use the Enterprise Scan Tool*
  http://support.microsoft.com/?id=894193

F.5.6 Windows XP SP3-Specific Resources

- *Overview of Windows XP Service Pack 3*
  http://download.microsoft.com/download/6/8/7/687484ed-8174-496d-8db9-f02b40c12982/Overview%20of%20Windows%20XP%20Service%20Pack%203.pdf

- Knowledge Base Article 936929, *Information about Windows XP Service Pack 3*
  http://support.microsoft.com/?id=936929

- Windows XP Service Packs
  http://technet.microsoft.com/en-us/windows/bb410118.aspx

F.6 Other Web-Based Resources

- *How Windows Server 2003's Software Restriction Policies Improve Security*
  http://www.windowsecurity.com/articles/windows_2003_restriction_policies_security.html

- *National Industrial Security Program Operating Manual*, DoD 5220.22-M, by the Department of Defense
  http://www.dtic.mil/whs/directives/corres/html/522022m.htm

- National Security Agency Security Recommendation Guides for Windows XP
  http://www.nsa.gov/snac/downloads_winxp.cfm

- *Searching and Seizing Computers and Obtaining Electronic Evidence in Criminal Investigations*, by the Department of Justice
  http://www.cybercrime.gov/s&smanual2002.htm

- Windows XP Resource Center
  http://labmice.techtarget.com/windowsxp/default.htm

- WinXPnews
  http://www.winxpnews.com/

Appendix G—Acronyms and Abbreviations

Selected acronyms and abbreviations used in the guide are defined below.

3DES	Triple Data Encryption Standard
ACE	Access Control Entry
ACL	Access Control List
AD	Active Directory
AES	Advanced Encryption Standard
AP	Access Point
AS	Authentication Service
BIOS	Basic Input/Output System
CCE	Common Configuration Enumeration
CD	Compact Disk
CHAP	Challenge Handshake Authentication Protocol
CIFS	Common Internet File System
CIS	Center for Internet Security
CS	Client/Server
DCOM	Distributed Component Object Model
DEP	Data Execution Prevention
DES	Data Encryption Standard
DESX	Extended Data Encryption Standard
DHCP	Dynamic Host Configuration Protocol
DHS	Department of Homeland Security
DIMS	Digital Identity Management Service
DISA	Defense Information Systems Agency
DLL	Dynamic Link Library
DNS	Domain Name System
DoS	Denial of Service
DRA	Data Recovery Agent
DTC	Distributed Transaction Coordinator
ECM	Enterprise Configuration Manager
EFS	Encrypting File System
e-mail	Electronic mail
FAT	File Allocation Table
FDCC	Federal Desktop Core Configuration
FEK	File Encryption Key
FIPS	Federal Information Processing Standards
FISMA	Federal Information Security Management Act
FTP	File Transfer Protocol
FUS	Fast User Switching
GB	Gigabyte
GINA	Graphical Identification and Authentication
GPMC	Group Policy Management Console

GPO	Group Policy Object
GUI	Graphical User Interface
HKLM	HKEY_Local_Machine
HTML	Hypertext Markup Language
HTTP	HyperText Transfer Protocol
HTTPS	HTTP Over SSL
ICF	Internet Connection Firewall
ICMP	Internet Control Message Protocol
ICS	Internet Connection Sharing
IE	Internet Explorer
IE7	Internet Explorer version 7
IETF	Internet Engineering Task Force
IIS	Internet Information Services
IKE	Internet Key Exchange
IM	Instant Messaging
IP	Internet Protocol
IPsec	IP Security
IRC	Internet Relay Chat
IT	Information Technology
ITL	Information Technology Laboratory
L2TP	Layer 2 Tunneling Protocol
LAN	Local Area Network
LM	LanManager
MBSA	Microsoft Baseline Security Analyzer
MMC	Microsoft Management Console
MS	Microsoft
MTU	Maximum Transmission Unit
NAP	Network Access Protection
NAT	Network Address Translation
NetBT	NetBIOS over TCP/IP
NIC	Network Interface Card
NIST	National Institute of Standards and Technology
NSA	National Security Agency
NTFS	NT File System
NTLM	NT LanManager
NTP	Network Time Protocol
NVD	National Vulnerability Database
NX	No Execute
OMB	Office of Management and Budget
OS	Operating System
OU	Organizational Unit
P2P	Peer-to-Peer
PIN	Personal Identification Number
PKI	Public Key Infrastructure

PPTP	Point-to-Point Tunneling Protocol
QoS	Quality of Service
RA	Remote Assistance
RC	Release Candidate
RCE	Route Cache Entry
RDP	Remote Desktop Protocol
RFC	Request for Comment
RIS	Remote Installation Service
RPC	Remote Procedure Call
RSVP	Resource Reservation Protocol
SACL	System Access Control List
SAM	Security Accounts Manager
SCAP	Security Content Automation Protocol
SID	Security Identify
SMB	Server Message Block
SMS	Systems Management Server
SMTP	Simple Mail Transport Protocol
SNMP	Simple Network Management Protocol
SOHO	Small Office Home Office
SP	Service Pack
SP2	Service Pack 2
SP3	Service Pack 3
SQL	Structured Query Language
SR	Service Release
SSDP	Simple Service Discovery Protocol
SSH	Secure Shell
SSID	Service Set Identifier
SSL	Secure Sockets Layer
SUS	Software Update Services
TCP	Transmission Control Protocol
TCP/IP	Transmission Control Protocol/Internet Protocol
TGS	Ticket-Granting Service
TLS	Transport Layer Security
UDP	User Datagram Protocol
UI	User Interface
UPnP	Universal Plug and Play
UPS	Uninterruptible Power Supply
URL	Uniform Resource Locator
US-CERT	United States Computer Emergency Readiness Team
VBS	Visual Basic Script
VoIP	Voice over IP
VPN	Virtual Private Network
WebDAV	Web Distributed Authoring and Versioning
WEP	Wired Equivalent Privacy

Wi-Fi	Wireless Fidelity
WPA	Wi-Fi Protected Access
WPA2	Wi-Fi Protected Access Version 2
WUS	Windows Update Services
WSUS	Windows Server Update Services

www.ingramcontent.com/pod-product-compliance
Lightning Source LLC
Chambersburg PA
CBHW080257180526
45167CB00006B/2568